Charles T. Robinson's

NATIVE NEW ENGLAND

The Long Journey

Illustrations by B. Turek Robinson

Covered Bridge Press

7 Adamsdale Road

North Attleborough, MA 02760

ISBN 0-924771-64-X

10 9 8 7 6 5 4 3 2 1

Library of Congress Cataloging-in-Publication Data

Robinson, Charles Turek, 1962-
    Native New England : the long journey / Charles Turek Robinson ;
illustrated by B. Turek Robinson
        p.   cm.
    Includes bibliographical references.
    ISBN 0-924771-64-X (paper)
    1. Indians of North America—New England—History.   I. Title.
E78.N5R63   1996
974'.01—dc20   96-11621
                                                                                      CIP

Critical Acclaim for Mr. Robinson's Previous Books and Articles on New England History and Folklore

"Robinson's (work) is excellent...The author has done a good job of researching and presenting his material...."
—Joe Citro, PBS Radio, WVPR Vermont

"...(none of the other books in this review) hold a candle...to Robinson's unembellished, deadpan reporting...."
—Geoffrey Elan, *Yankee*

"From the depths of obscurity, the prehistoric Indians come alive with insights into their daily activities and traditions, and accounts of their myths and legends."
—James McDonald, *The Providence Journal-Bulletin*

"...writes in a straightforward, no-nonsense fashion...no fluff...."
—Paul Kandarian, City Editor, *Taunton Daily Gazette*

"...strives for perfection."
—Paula Kerr, *The Fall River Herald*

"Most people can tell you a good deal about their hometowns. But Charles Robinson is unique. He can go back thousands of years to tell you about his."
—Fred Lewis, *Brockton Enterprise*

Acknowledgements

For the knowledge they have shared and/or the inspiration they have afforded, I am profoundly grateful to the following people, each of whom has played a substantive role in the creation of *Native New England: The Long Journey.*

For his patience and forbearance – and for his valuable creative input – I am indebted to my publisher, Chuck Durang of Covered Bridge Press.

For the wisdom he has shared, and for the friendship he has offered, I am deeply grateful to O'ee-Tash Round-Tree of the Ponkopoag Tribe.

Profound thanks to Robert S. Sharples for allowing me research access to his New England artifact collection – and for taking the time to show me numerous archaeological sites in southeastern Massachusetts. Bob has been a teacher and a friend.

I thank Deborah Cahoon Didick for sharing her vast knowledge of Native American legends and folklore. I also thank her – and her husband, Richard – for support and friendship of a most precious sort.

I am grateful to Phyllis Dupere, who has shared her research in the area of Algonquin cooking and food preparation. Additionally, throughout the course of this book project and earlier ones, Phyllis has unreservedly offered her assistance and friendship.

Thanks to E. Otis Dyer, Jr. and Dick Georgia – as well as all other members of the 350th Anniversary Steering Committee of Rehoboth, Massachusetts – for arts grant funding of my earlier book, *Asleep Beneath The Meadows,* which eventually evolved into the present book.

I am also grateful to Kevin Cordeiro for sharing his vast knowledge of prehistoric New England artifact typology.

Both the author and the publisher are extremely grateful to Don Langevin — for his thoughtful and innovative work on the layout and design of this book.

Dedication

To Mendell and Beatrice Robinson,
whose love and support are the foundation of it all.

Contents

Preface

How long have human beings occupied New England? The answer may astound you. If you were to guess that Indians have occupied New England for, say, ten centuries – or a thousand years – your guess would be short by more than one hundred centuries. In fact, from carbon-dated artifactual remains, archaeologists now know that Native American people have inhabited the region for about one hundred and twenty centuries – actually, for a little over twelve thousand years.

The people of ancient New England have been swallowed by the ages; they have disappeared into a past so shadowy, dim, and distant that, to us, it is hard to imagine that it ever even mattered. Countless lives, actions, inventions, conflicts, marriages, births, deaths, tragedies, joys, hopes, failures, and dreams remain forever enshrouded in the mists of vast antiquity.

Yet, in New England and anywhere else on the planet, it is possible for us to glance backward across the ages. Archaeology is the business of building bridges back across time. The people lost to time have left part of themselves behind. Their remains and artifacts, when properly recovered and pieced together, and when supplemented with botanical, geological, and zoological studies aimed at reconstructing ancient environments, afford us glimpses into the human dramas and struggles that preceded us. In looking into the past of any human culture, we are really looking into ourselves. The human experience is one of continuum. In learning where we came from, we learn where we are – and where we might yet like to go.

My interests in human antiquity are broad. There is scarcely an ancient culture that does not intrigue me, for I believe that the experiences of all peoples in all times can tell us much about the business of living. Yet, I must admit a special affinity for the ancient cultures that existed right in my own region. I have lived in New England for my entire life, and I have developed a deep and insatiable curiosity concerning the textured, colorful, and strikingly beautiful Native American cultures that, for millennia, flourished in this part of the country.

What were they like, the people who, for ages, roamed and hunted and camped in the forests, valleys, and mountains of New England? How did they live, and how did their lives change and evolve over numerous generations and centuries? What technologies did they utilize? What did they wear, and where did they sleep? What and how did they worship? How did they relate to one another? Once our ancestors reached New England, how did they relate to us? And why, ultimately, did our arrival mean their demise?

I hope this book will begin to answer these questions. I hope that it will raise even more, and that others will be inspired to wonder.

Charles Turek Robinson
Rehoboth, Massachusetts
March 18, 1996

Chapter One

The Paleo-Indian Period
10,500 B.C.- 7,000 B.C.

BACKGROUND

The region known as New England was formally settled by English colonists in 1620. That seems so very long ago. But was it? What is a mere three or four hundred years when compared with over twelve thousand? Archaeological evidence indicates that human beings have occupied New England since 10,500 B.C. In other words, people were living in the region for an almost incomprehensible amount of time before recorded New World history. By the time Columbus reached America over five hundred years ago, human habitation in New England was already more than one hundred centuries old!

And yet, in the chronology of American prehistory, people first arrived in New England relatively late. Small bands of nomadic hunter-gatherers were already living in the northwestern portion of America by as early as 20,000-30,000 B.C., and perhaps even earlier. They were migrants from Asia who had crossed over the Bering Strait into Alaska (because much of the world's water was still locked up in Late Pleistocene glaciers at this time, ocean levels were significantly lower, and the Bering Strait was probably a now-submerged land bridge that connected Siberia and the North American continent).

These ancient Asian nomads were the ancestors of all subsequent Native American groups. Over many thousands of years, their descendants migrated southward and eastward. By about 10,500 B.C., some of them reached New England, not long after the formidable Wisconsin glacier – the last of New England's Pleistocene glaciers – had begun to retreat in response to a warming climate.

These first arrivals are called "Paleo-Indians" by archaeologists. They occupy a dim and distant place in New England's past. We know much less about them than about the local natives of millennia

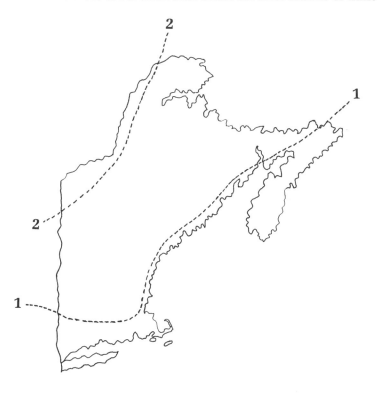

Map delineating glacial retreat in Late Pleistocene New England: Line #1 shows the edge of the glacial ice sheet at about 11,500 B.C. Line #2 shows the position of the ice sheet's edge at about 10,500 B.C., by which time continued warming had caused the glacier to retreat much farther northward.

later – the Woodland Indians – whom the colonists met when they first arrived. However, archaeological excavations have yielded at least some clues of Paleo-Indian life and culture, which lasted for some 3,500 years, spanning the period from 10,500 B.C. to about 7,000 B.C.

CLIMATE, FLORA, AND FAUNA

For thousands of years, New England had slumbered under the Wisconsin Glacier, whose ice once stood more than a mile thick over the region. By about 13,000 B.C., the glacier had begun to melt in response to warming temperatures. The edge of the ice sheet retreated northward, and, by 11,500 B.C., the southernmost portion of New England was open to the development of plant and animal communities. Within another thousand years, the glacier had retreated as far north as the St. Lawrence River area, exposing a significant amount of terrain, which now offered enough new flora and fauna to attract the first humans to the region.

New England of the Paleo-Indian period would have been unrecognizable to us. Our modern hardwood forest, with a predominance of such trees as oak, beech, and maple, did not yet exist, since the climate was significantly cooler. The earliest vegetation was tundra grass and flora, soon followed by a mostly evergreen forest of spruce and then pine as the climate continued to warm, especially in more southerly parts of the region. Northern portions of New England that were closer to the edge of the still-retreating ice sheet (like Maine, for instance) remained desolate tundra grassland until about the end of the period. "Within a few hundred miles of the glacial base, only the tundra could survive. Stunted clumps of spruce and fir rose above a scattered growth of grasses, sages, and willows. Today, Cape Cod gives something of the feeling of those early times (Wilbur: 2)."

Vast stretches of southeastern New England may have resembled this barren, lifeless wasteland at about 13,500 B.C., when the glacier had begun to melt and retreat. Soon, however, this wet, gnarled, empty landscape would begin to sprout tundra flora.

*With the glacier retreating farther and farther
northward out of New England, the warming
environment gave rise to tundra flora and, eventually, an
evergreen forest setting that attracted large grazing
animals like the caribou and mastodon.*

3

However, in more southerly areas, including Rhode Island and Massachusetts, the evergreen forest thrived, and, as the climate continued to become more temperate, the conifers eventually began to mix with some oak and birch, though evergreens remained predominant.

Since much of the world's water was still locked up in continental ice sheets, ocean levels, compared to those of today, remained significantly lower throughout the Paleo-Indian period, exposing substantial portions of the continental shelf, with only a gradual sea elevation that would continue for millennia. Paleo-Indians would have viewed Martha's Vineyard and Nantucket as large hills on the landscape, rather than islands.

Similarly, the fauna of the Paleo-Indian period was completely unlike that of today. To a great extent, it consisted of large migratory game animals such as caribou and the now-extinct mastodon (a forerunner of the modern elephant, these huge, tusked, shaggy creatures were once as common in North America as the elephant is common in India today). These large Pleistocene game animals grazed on tundra grasses or browsed on lichens in the evergreen forest. Creatures like caribou and mastodons attracted Paleo-Indians to the New England region and served as one of their primary food sources.

SETTLEMENT PATTERNS

Archaeological remains, including site distributions and artifact concentrations, indicate that Paleo-Indians wandered New England in small bands, each composed of four or five families, totalling perhaps twenty or thirty people per band. Bands were nomadic; their movements likely depended on those of the migratory big game herds. However, though bands probably moved about without any restriction early on in the period, successful subsistence probably required an eventual controlled dispersion of people, in the form of

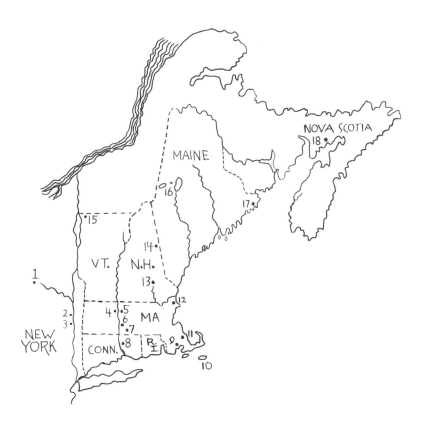

This map delineates some of New England's better known Paleo-Indian campsites and artifact recovery sites, from which archaeologists have recovered stone tools and weapons that tell us something of Paleo-Indian settlement and sustenance patterns.

To right: By 10,500 B.C., small bands of nomadic hunters had begun to move into New England, probably in pursuit of game animals like the mastodon. These first Indian arrivals to New England are called "Paleo-Indians" by archaeologists.

each band marking its own territory and excluding others from it, so that the game resources of any particular area would not become over-exploited:

Deliberate spacing and territorial restrictions probably developed as those first bands of Paleo-Indians grew and split, or were added to by others drifting into New England.... A successful subsistence strategy would have depended on a neighborly maintenance of boundaries.... It seems likely that each band maintained a territory that its members considered their own, moving about within it according to the movements of the big game animals.... They probably had polite understandings with adjacent bands regarding territorial rights...

Snow: 150-152

Within their respective territories, bands remained highly mobile. While there was some seasonal regularity to the broader movements of the large game herds, local movements could be erratic and frequent. Therefore, Paleo-Indian campsites were rudimentary and were probably never occupied for considerable periods at a time. Camps were often situated on elevations, where a commanding view would allow hunters to monitor the movements of the surrounding game herds. At Assowompsett Lake in Middleboro, Massachusetts, for instance, where archaeologists unearthed Paleo-Indian remains dating back more than 10,000 years, a small band of Paleo-Indians apparently pitched camp on top of a large sand dune at the north shore of Lake Assowompsett, elevated about twelve meters above the present lake. Here, the Indians had a good view of the surrounding countryside, as well as access to the lake's fresh water and the prey it attracted.

While there is no surviving material in the Paleo-Indian archaeological record that delineates housing, we can make assumptions based on ethnographic comparison with similar but more recent hunter-gatherer cultures in other parts of the world. Shelter at campsites apparently consisted of simple brush-framed huts covered with animal skins – one for each of the four or five nuclear families in the band – that could be easily dismantled after a brief period of hunting in the area. Sometimes, natural caves or rock shelters were also used for temporary cover. Inhabitants roasted their meat over open hearths, and they set up temporary workshop areas where they crafted stone tools and weapons. Archaeologists have located a few of these very ancient and rudimentary campsites, and it is likely that more of them lie deeply buried in certain undeveloped parts of New England – a premise supported by the occasional appearance of a timeworn Paleo-Indian stone projectile point in some plowed field or another.

BAND INTERACTION

While Paleo-Indians apparently moved in small bands that were relatively independent from one another, ethnographic comparison with other similar hunting cultures would suggest a certain amount of probable interaction:

Ethnographically known bands of this sort are always exogamous....That is, band members always look to other bands for mates. Moreover, among hunting cultures like the Paleo-Indians, newly married couples probably normally resided with the man's band. This patrilocal residence rule ensured that men stayed within the hunting ranges and with the hunting partners with which they were most familiar. At the same time, bands maintained good relations with adjacent bands by virtue of having kin contacts with them through their female members....

(Since some Paleo-Indian sites have yielded artifacts made of a variety of cherts indigenous to widely scattered geographical areas), it seems unlikely that any band of Paleo-Indians would have ranged far enough to quarry all of those materials. Therefore, we have to conclude that some trade in finished products was going on during the Paleo-Indian period....

The establishment of trading partnerships between members of different bands is common and supplements the binding power of intermarriage.... It could well be that it was women, with their strong blood connections to other bands, who were the primary conduits of exchange. Bands living in territories poor in chert resources would probably have found other materials to exchange for chert with other bands.

Snow: 139-141

Thus, while the limited resources of any particular area might have required each small band to travel alone within its territory and politely deny other bands access, it seems quite apparent that there were occasional multi-band encampments in which several bands briefly gathered together to exchange gifts (especially cherts, highly prized for making stone weapons) that would reinforce territorial understandings. "Trade" among Paleo-Indians, then, might be better defined as diplomatic gift-exchange. At these brief multi-band encampments, inter-marriages quite probably also took place.

The Bull Brook Site near Ipswich, Massachusetts, which is situated on a kame terrace about twelve meters above modern sea level, is one of New England's most important and well-recognized Paleo-Indian sites. It has produced archaeological evidence which tends to support the premise that bands occasionally camped together for brief social events of gift exchange and inter-marriage. Artifact assemblages were distributed in forty-five concentrations, each of which averaged 4.5-6.0 meters in diameter, about the size that would be consistent with one nuclear family. The concentrations were arranged in a large semi-circle, and this distinct pattern suggests a simultaneous encampment of forty-five nuclear families, or about two hundred twenty-five people – many more than would have normally traveled together. Quite possibly, then, Bull Brook was the scene of a temporary multiband encampment where gift exchange and marriage took place over 10,000 years ago – after which the gathering broke up, and each band headed off alone into its own hunting territory.

FOOD PROCUREMENT AND HUNTING TECHNOLOGY

The probable reliance of Paleo-Indians on large Pleistocene game animals is what some researchers call a "focal subsistence strategy," as opposed to a "diffuse subsistence strategy," which involves the exploitation of many diverse resources. While some researchers have begun to suggest that Paleo-Indians may have exploited a variety of food sources, the current consensus still seems to be that Paleo-Indians were primarily hunters of large game.

Paleo-Indians occupied New England at a time when the tundra environment was rapidly evolving into a predominantly evergreen forest setting as the climate continued to warm. Other than large game animals, most resources were probably too sparse or were shifting too quickly with the changing environment to be reliable. New England did not yet offer dependable annual bounties of such foods as edible nuts, fish runs, or shellfish. Of course, Paleo-Indians may have occasionally fished or eaten plants, but these types of food resources were not yet available with any sort of stable seasonal regularity, and the agriculture of New England's later Indian culture was still thousands of years away.

The prototypical assortment of tools and weapons recovered from ancient Paleo-Indian sites seems to reflect this focal subsistence dependence on large game animals. In the Paleo-Indian material archaeological record, there is a distinct absence of stone fishing weights or stone tools for grinding plants and seeds, while there is an abundance of projectile points for spearing game, stone knives for cutting meat, and stone scrapers for fleshing animal hides.

The illustration on the preceding two pages depicts a typical Paleo-Indian campsite. Because Paleo-Indian bands were frequently on the move in pursuit of game, camps were rudimentary and were probably not occupied for long periods. The sapling-framed, skin-covered shelter at the upper left could be quickly assembled and disassembled and probably housed a single family. Each campsite probably accommodated four or five such nuclear families, totalling perhaps twenty to thirty people per travelling band.

There is little doubt that Paleo-Indian hunters took a great deal of pride in their stoneworking. Their projectile points, for instance, were delicately flaked and chipped into amazingly precise and symmetrical forms, and they represent some of the finest known prehistoric projectiles in the world. They were sometimes "fluted" for hafting and averaged in length from 1 3/4 to 3 3/4 inches. The larger specimens were apparently utilized as spear points for larger game like caribou and mastodons. The smaller projectile points suggest that these people also speared smaller game on occasion – including birds and waterfowl.

At no point did Paleo-Indians utilize the bow and arrow. They did, however, employ the atlatl stick, a hand-held, stone-weighted spear launcher that significantly improved projectile range and accuracy. Separating a caribou or mastodon from its herd, Paleo-Indian hunters probably drove the animal over a cliff or into the mire of a swamp, where it was trapped and more easily slaughtered. To minimize risks, hunters may have selected younger, lighter animals when mastodons were the prey (some varieties of mastodon could, as adults, be as large as fourteen feet high, rendering them formidable, dangerous targets for human hunters). There is no skeletal evidence, as exists in western America, that Paleo-Indians in New England practiced "Pleistocene overkill," in which entire herds of large game were driven over large cliffs for the sake of taking just one or two needed animals.

While the Paleo-Indian culture is far too ancient for a sound determination of gender roles, it seems reasonable to conclude, based on ethnographic comparison with comparable hunting cultures, that adult males, along with their older sons acting in learning roles, were responsible for hunting, while females and their daughters tended to the removing of meat from carcasses and fleshing the hides for use as clothing and shelter covering. However, in the present writer's opinion, the participation of some women in the hunt cannot be ruled out with certainty. Considering their highly mobile lifestyle, Paleo-Indian women, like the men, were undoubtedly of

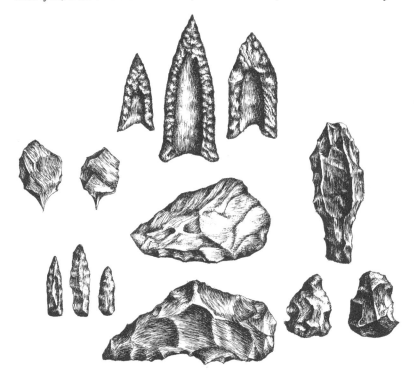

The illustration above shows a typical array of stone tools found at New England campsites dating to the Paleo-Indian period (Ca. 10,500-7,000 B.C.), including spearpoints, knives, drills, and scrapers. Clearly, this prototypical assortment of Paleo-Indian stone tools reflects a focal subsistence strategy on large game animals. Although Paleo-Indians undoubtedly sometimes also fished and ate plants, the absence at their sites of stone fishing weights and stone tools for grinding plants and seeds suggests that such resources were not yet available in New England with any sort of stable seasonal regularity. Of course, this limited tundra environment would change quite dramatically for New England's later Indian cultures, who would eventually enjoy a warmer climate and a deciduous forest setting rich in diverse resources.

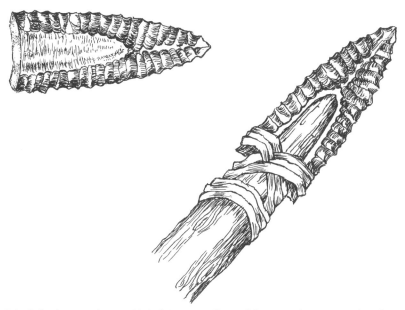

Indian cultures of later periods, were apparently not people who were largely river-oriented. Their frequent movements in following game herds across the landscape were probably much better facilitated by terrestrial foot travel.

Paleo-Indian hunters took great pride in their stone-working, and their projectile points were chipped into very precise, symmetrical forms. As shown here, they were often "fluted" to facilitate hafting to a wooden spear shaft.

exceptional and robust physical condition; some of them (perhaps those without children) may have successfully joined male hunting parties in stalking and taking down large game.

TRANSPORTATION

There is no archaeological evidence to suggest that canoes were commonly in use during this early period (though rudimentary wooden watercraft may have been occasionally employed to traverse bodies of water). As large game hunters who lived in a rapidly changing environment where predictable fish runs were not yet reliable seasonal events, the Paleo-Indians, unlike the New England

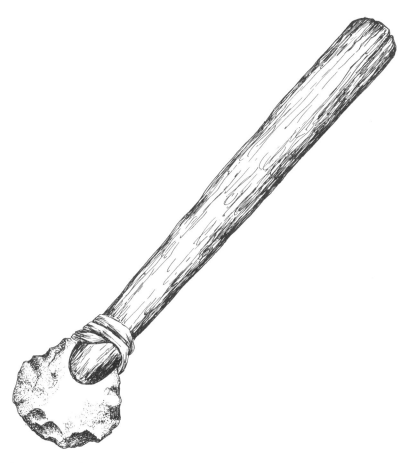

A stone scraper, utilized in removing fat and tissue from animal skins and furs. As with many Paleo-Indian stone tools, this specimen was tightly hafted to a wooden handle with strips of rawhide or strong reeds.

APPEARANCE AND DRESS

While stone artifacts survive for millennia, other cultural artifacts (made of organic materials such as wood, bone, or leather) usually do not, especially in New England's highly acidic soil. Still, we can make some educated assumptions. For instance, we can surmise as to how Paleo-Indians dressed, based on what we know of their envi-

ronment and survival skills. It seems apparent that they wore animal skins and furs, as well as footwear wrought from hide, perhaps fur-lined in colder weather. In attempting to further envision their physical appearance, we can also make assumptions based on what we know of their derivation from Asian stock, even though New England has yielded no skeletal remains from this very ancient period. It seems reasonable to conclude that Paleo-Indians had

Mongoloid characteristics, with straight black hair, slanted eyelids, wide cheekbones, and shovel-shaped incisor teeth. They were, in other words, an attractive Asian people.

NON-MATERIAL CULTURAL TRAITS

Many non-material facets of Paleo-Indian culture remain completely obscure. For instance, though the archaeological and historical records tell us something of Indian religious belief during the later New England cultural periods of the Archaic and, especially, the Woodland Indians, there is no surviving material delineating Paleo-Indian religion or world view. We can only wonder, based on our knowledge of Paleo-Indian reliance on game animals (and on the physical environment in general), if these people deified natural forces and thereby attempted to manipulate them in their favor with various rituals. Like most ancient cultures, they very likely did so.

Similarly, we cannot know for certain whether or not individual bands sometimes had designated "leaders," though there is no evidence to suggest anything other than egalitarianism (in contrast to the region's much later Native cultures) at such an early period. Considering that each band was apparently small and highly nomadic, it is hard to imagine the need for any formal authority structuring, though elder members of the group (considering the familial nature of bands) or those exhibiting exceptional strength or character were perhaps afforded especial respect, and, to some extent, may have sometimes been relied upon by the rest of the band during times of trouble. Similarly, if particular members of the band were entrusted with the management of religious ritual, the importance of this function may have afforded them especial prominence.

CONCLUSIONS

Many other facts concerning Paleo-Indian culture – given the vast antiquity within which these early people remain enshrouded – remain lost to the passage of numerous centuries since these Indians once wandered ancient New England. We cannot even be certain which parts of New England attracted the greatest number of these ancient nomads. Their movements were apparently dependent on those of the game animals, and their temporary campsites were widely scattered, some of them quite far inland.

However, there is a possibility that higher concentrations of Paleo-Indian artifacts lie off of our coast. The sea level was significantly lower during this period, and numerous recoveries of mastodon teeth in fishing nets indicate that vast portions of continental shelf were exposed and habitable during Paleo-Indian times. Many of these early Indians may have camped and hunted on the extensive coastal plains (where food was perhaps more plentiful) that have long since been obliterated by rising waters. Thus, it is

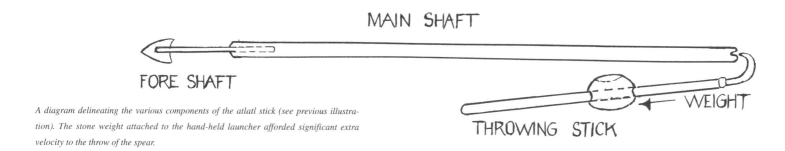

A diagram delineating the various components of the atlatl stick (see previous illustration). The stone weight attached to the hand-held launcher afforded significant extra velocity to the throw of the spear.

possible that the relics of a Paleo-Indian "Atlantis," of sorts, lie sunken fathoms deep off the New England coastline.

The decline and end of Paleo-Indian life patterns in New England took place about 7,000 B.C., by which time the large Pleistocene game animals on which these people apparently depended had either migrated north or had died off in response to further warming of the climate and its attendant changes in flora (and perhaps also in response to being over-hunted, a premise that is the topic of much debate). Subsequently, local Indians would have to dramatically readapt to a new type of forest environment, heralding the beginning of the Archaic Indian Period, which we will address in the next chapter.

Despite our vague knowledge of this very early culture, the beautifully wrought Paleo-Indian tools and weapons that have survived the millennia communicate much about New England's first Indians and their similarities to modern mankind. They sought out shelter and sustenance. They interacted, married, and raised children. They strived for new tools and technologies. They took pride in their accomplishments. They dreamed and they planned. Most importantly, they survived.

To left: Typical clothing likely worn by Paleo-Indians in colder weather, consisting of layered animal hides which, in winter, were probably supplemented with fur linings. As noted previously, animal skins were also employed as covering for sapling-framed shelters, as seen at left.

As the New England climate continued to warm, the mostly evergreen and tundra setting of Paleo-Indian days gradually gave way to a northward expanding hardwood forest which eventually featured more modern animal species. Indian adaptation to this newly evolving forest environment would characterize the Archaic Indian Period.

16

Chapter Two

The Archaic Period
7,000-500 B.C.
OVERVIEW

By about 7,000 B.C., as the New England climate continued to warm, the evergreen forest had begun to mix with a good amount of oak and other warmth-loving deciduous species in more southerly parts of the region. In time, a deciduous hardwood forest would begin to predominate over southern New England, and hardwoods would also eventually begin to mingle with conifers in the north. As the tundra had retreated farther northward out of New England, so had the grassy tundra ranges on which many large Pleistocene animals grazed. Big game like caribou and mastodons disappeared from the region and were being replaced by more modern animals better suited to the changing climate and flora. With this gradual shift in environment came new Indian life patterns that eventually supplanted those of the previous culture.

The Archaic period spanned some 6,500 years, beginning about 7,000 B.C. and terminating with the emergence of Woodland-Ceramic (agricultural/pottery-making) culture about 500 B.C. Archaic Indians were of the same Asian stock as the Paleo-Indians (some were their descendants, while others may have been new Indian bands that moved into the region and mingled with the older groups). Their culture in New England featured some variation in different parts of the region and saw various changes over many generations. What most distinguished them from their Paleo-Indian predecessors were their new settlement patterns and food procurement technologies (some perhaps imported from other parts of the country, others local in origin) that continuously evolved in response to a warming climate and its attendant changes in flora and wildlife.

SETTLEMENT AND SUBSISTENCE PATTERNS

Like the preceding Paleo-Indians, Archaic people were nomadic, moving about New England in relatively small and dispersed bands for a good part of each year. As in the preceding period, each band probably had its own general territory to which it restricted its movements. As the Archaic period progressed, some territories eventually became home to sets of bands which, while moving independently of one another in the fall and winter months, apparently came together for relatively large, multi-band spring and summer encampments, as will be later discussed in greater detail.

As the weather continued to warm and the new forest gradually took hold, Archaic Indians began to adapt themselves to the changing environment. No longer dependent on wandering large game herds, Archaic people developed fresh technology for hunting and trapping New England's newer, smaller and less mobile species of game, which included increasing numbers of white-tail deer, black bear, moose, and turkey, among others. As marine life also diversified in response to the improving climate, Archaic Indians perfected ways to fish and to spear seals and whales. Additionally, as the new forest of deciduous hardwoods continued to spread over time, there were new seasonal bounties of edible nuts, roots, and berries that Archaic people could incorporate into their diet.

Indian adaptation to New England's newer and more diverse resources became increasingly skillful as the period progressed and the environment continued to stabilize (in other words, Archaic Indians developed a "diffuse" subsistence strategy, involving the exploitation of many diverse resources, in contrast to the "focal" subsistence strategy of the earlier Paleo-Indians, who seemingly specialized, to a significant extent, on a single primary resource of game meat). Archaic bands gradually learned which areas were best

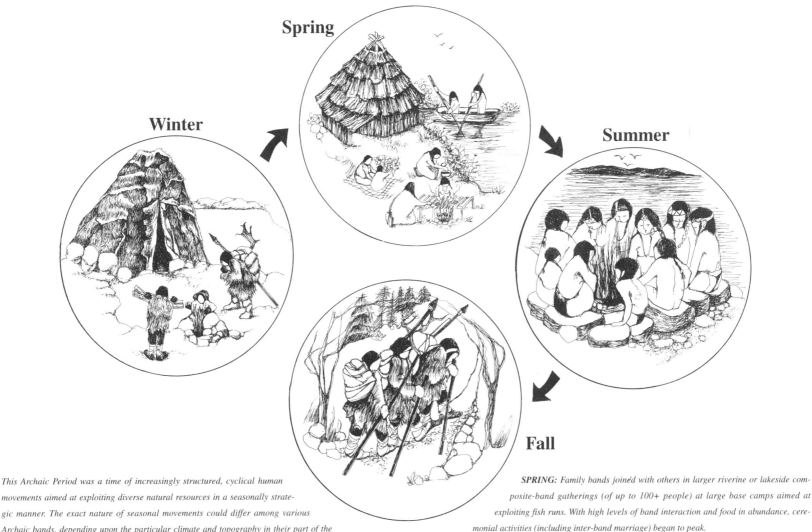

Spring

Winter

Summer

Fall

This Archaic Period was a time of increasingly structured, cyclical human movements aimed at exploiting diverse natural resources in a seasonally strategic manner. The exact nature of seasonal movements could differ among various Archaic bands, depending upon the particular climate and topography in their part of the region. A typical Archaic settlement pattern – common in southern New England but also seen, perhaps in different variations, among some Archaic bands in other New England territories – seems to have been structured in the following manner, with bands returning to the same sites year after year, following the cycle of the seasons:

WINTER: *Small, separate family bands spent their winters thinly spread out in various inland game-hunting areas.*

SPRING: *Family bands joined with others in larger riverine or lakeside composite-band gatherings (of up to 100+ people) at large base camps aimed at exploiting fish runs. With high levels of band interaction and food in abundance, ceremonial activities (including inter-band marriage) began to peak.*

SUMMER: *Groups sometimes moved on to favorite coastal spots, where they set up coastal camps and supplemented their diet with shellfish.*

FALL: *Large, multi-band encampments broke up, and small family bands set off separately for an inland trek to winter hunting grounds.*

exploited at different times of the year. Spring began to offer dependable fish runs in many rivers. Summer eventually meant large beds of shellfish at the coast. Winter brought a high concentration of small game in the inland forest. Predictable, seasonal cycles of human movement developed, ones that were more structured and less frequent than those of the preceding Paleo-Indians, whose movements, as we have noted, were most likely dependent on those of the large game herds they were following.

Archaic Indian bands eventually began to use utilize favorite locales again and again, leaving a preferred site when resources became seasonally sparse and returning to it when they had regenerated. This development is especially evident for the middle and, even more, for the later part of the period (i.e. from about 4,000 B.C. onward), by which time Archaic people had fully adapted themselves to the new environment, which, at this point, included much of the same flora and fauna present in New England today.

Archaeological remains for the early part of the Archaic period are extremely scarce, and we know very little of early Archaic culture (one possible reason: because the ocean level was still significantly lower during the early part of the period, a good number of early Archaic campsites may have been subsequently submerged as the sea level continued to rise. A second possible reason: as the glacier and its associated tundra environment retreated farther northward out of a warming New England, some early Archaic Indians may have followed the dwindling, migrating large game herds up into Canada). Remains for the middle and, especially, the later part of the Archaic period, however, are much more common, and from these ancient artifact deposits archaeologists have discerned distinct patterns of Archaic movement and subsistence.

As indicated, the middle and, especially, the later parts of the Archaic period saw Indian bands moving in regular, seasonally cycli-cal patterns in their various New England territories. Depending on specific topography and climate, precise patterns of seasonal movement varied in different parts of New England. In many parts of the region, it seems that Archaic Indians were spending the fall and winter months in inland game hunting areas, spread out in small, separate family bands. When spring brought the first run of fish, however, family bands often joined together with others from nearby areas in larger, composite-band gatherings (of up to a hundred or so people) at preferred lakeside or riverine fishing sites. In some areas, with the arrival of summer, groups moved on to favorite coastal spots, where they could enjoy cool ocean breezes and supplement their diet with shellfish. It was during these fair-weather gatherings, when food was in abundance and family groups were able to readily interact, that recreational and ceremonial activities (including marriage) were most likely at their peak. As fall and colder weather set in, these larger groups apparently broke up, and individual family bands set off on their own, often for an inland trek to winter hunting grounds.

There is little evidence to strongly suggest any permanent, year-round villages in Archaic New England. Without the application of agriculture (which would not develop in Native New England until somewhat later), any particular area was limited in its available food supply. Archaic Indians did not have domesticated animals (with the possible exception of the wolf dog, which may have been used for hunting and as a reserve food source). Aside from the smoking of fish, these people knew no method for preserving food; therefore, settlements could not maintain large food supplies throughout the entire year.

However, there is evidence to suggest *semi-permanent* settlements in some parts of Archaic New England. As noted earlier, Archaic Indians had, by the middle and, especially, by the later parts of the period, become progressively adept at utilizing the region's resources in a seasonally strategic manner. In many parts of New

As the New England climate continued to warm and fish runs settled into reliable seasonal patterns, Archaic Indians became increasingly more river-oriented than their Paleo-Indian forebears.

20

England, this seasonal adaptation eventually resulted in the larger spring and/or summer gatherings described above, during which family bands gathered together at favorite riverine or lakeside sites to take advantage of fish runs at the precise time of the year they were available. Since food was in abundance at such times, these favorite, composite-band gathering places sometimes began to see relatively continuous occupation during the warmer parts of each year. Often utilized by the same groups season after season, these sites sometimes became semi-permanent, seasonal base camps of significant size (perhaps a hundred or so individuals, or about twenty-five families) where, in addition to fishing, inhabitants also engaged in "collecting and processing plant and animal products, wood-working, and a variety of other maintenance activities (Luedtke: 293)."

A striking example is to be found in southeastern Massachusetts, at Lake Assowompsett in Middleboro. Near the lake's north shore, under the direction of Dr. Maurice Robbins, the Cohannet Chapter of the Massachusetts Archaeological Society uncovered the impressive remains of a seasonal, late Archaic settlement which had accommodated a group of one hundred or so Indians who returned to the site every spring. Most significantly, the excavation revealed traces of seven large, circular wooden structures which had been substantively constructed of wooden posts and beams and had apparently been shingled with bark. The enclosures had ranged from thirty-three to sixty-six feet in diameter, and the largest had apparently served as a ceremonial lodge, since it contained eleven secondary human burials with associated stone grave goods. The smaller structures – which had doorways with side walls to keep out the wind – had probably served as dwellings. Radio-carbon dating of associated charcoal dated these impressive structural remains to about 2,300 B.C.

This intriguing Middleboro site – known to archaeologists as Wapanucket #6 – has important implications. The nature of the wooden structures had been substantial, confirming that some New England Indian bands, as the Archaic period progressed, were, within their respective territories, living an increasingly structured and settled sort of existence in seasonal, semi-permanent fair-weather base camps. In his site report, Dr. Robbins suggests the following late Archaic habitation pattern at Wapanucket #6:

> After a winter spent ranging in small family groups about the (inland) hunting territory to the north and west, the band would return, quite naturally, to this favored site on the shore of the great lake. Here they would find quantities of food readily available and here they would perform the ceremonies demanded by their culture. Those who had departed this life during the long winter would be brought here for burial. As the season advanced, the urge to enjoy the cool breezes of the seashore and to partake of the succulent shellfish to be found there could be satisfied by a short canoe trip by way of either the Nemasket and the Taunton River to Narragansett Bay or down the Mattapoisett River to Buzzard's Bay. Probably they would again gather at the lake in the fall of the year to pick up the stores of preserved (smoked) fish before dispersing for the long winter in the hunting territory. A possible clue to the size of this band lies in the size of their lodges and in the spaciousness of the ceremonial lodge. It would seem that a minimum of twenty persons might find accommodation in these large dwellings. If so, we may assume that this band was composed of at least six family groups, perhaps totalling more than a hundred individuals.
>
> Robbins 1959: 79

This Archaic wooden habitation structure was one of several that stood in an ancient fishing campsite situated – circa 2,300 B.C. – on the north shore of Lake Assowompsett in Middleboro, Massachusetts.

22

NEW TECHNOLOGIES

As noted earlier, the food procurement patterns of Archaic people became markedly different from those of the earlier Paleo-Indian culture, since large Pleistocene game animals had given way to smaller mammals better suited to the warming New England climate and its newly emerging deciduous forest. Archaic Indians employed new hunting technology to deal with the increasingly diversified population of more modern animal species.

For instance, as the climate continued to improve and fish runs settled into reliable seasonal patterns, Archaic people utilized a number of new fishing weights and lures crafted of stone, the most expertly wrought of which were the plummet-shaped stone sinkers that emerged during the middle Archaic. Harpoons – with wooden shafts and razor-sharp points made of wood or stone – came into use early on in the period and were employed in hunting seals and even whales, which were pursued in small but sea-worthy dugout canoes.

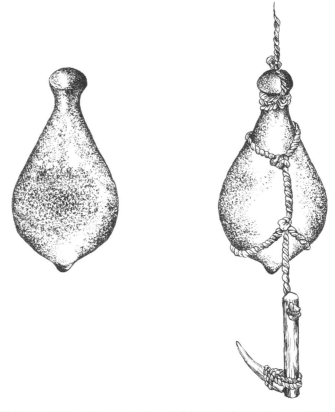

Middle Archaic Classic Plummet, also shown hafted with wooden hook. To attract fish, bait was probably smeared on the faces of this expertly-wrought stone lure.

Shellfish were not the only resource utilized by Archaic bands when visiting coastal sites, as this early Archaic harpoon suggests. Seals and whales were harpooned from dugout canoes.

Some Archaic bands, especially during the later part of the period, began to build fish weirs, perhaps the most innovative of primitive fishing technologies. In Boston, the striking remains of such a weir were discovered in 1913 during excavation for a subway. Known to archaeologists as the Boylston Street Fish Weir, this elaborate sub-aquatic trapping system was constructed in Boston-area waters (the Charles River estuary) about 2,000 B.C. It had consisted of a meshed enclosure beneath the water's surface, composed of some 65,000 wooden stakes entwined with brush. At high tide, large

23

Artist's rendering of a semi-permanent Archaic fishing base camp, based on lakeside archaeological excavations at Wapanucket #6, Middleboro, Massachusetts.

24

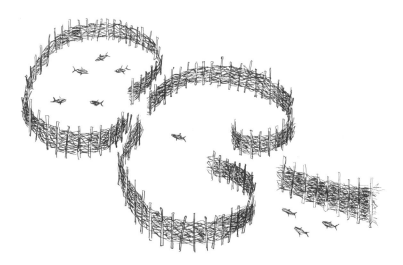

The late Archaic fish weir, a famous example of which is known to archaeologists in Boston. At high tide, large numbers of fish became entrapped within elaborate underwater meshed enclosures consisting of tens of thousands of wooden stakes entwined with brush.

pitted stone anvils for cracking nuts, and, during the later part of the period, they innovated stone mortars and pestles for grinding.

Supplementing these advances in food procurement technology were additional stone artifact forms that allowed Archaic Indians to take advantage of the many hardwoods offered by the new forest. New wood-working tools, which have been found in good numbers at many Archaic New England sites, included stone grooved axes, adzes, gouges and celts. Undoubtedly, these tools were used to manufacture wooden bowls and cups that have not survived the region's acidic soils. These new stone implements also played an important role in the manufacturing of dugout canoes, which, during this increasingly river-oriented period, were a very effective means of navigating New England's extensive river systems to reach interior camping, hunting and fishing grounds (no Archaic canoes survive. Undoubtedly, they were sturdy dugout craft, made by hollowing out large tree trunks with stone implements like the gouge).

numbers of fish were carried into the enclosure through a small opening and became entrapped within. It must have been good eating in that part of Archaic New England; below Boston-area waters, the Boylston Street Fish Weir covered an area of about three acres (the associated campsite, which was undoubtedly large, has not yet been located by archaeologists).

A most important development quite late in the period (about 1,700 B.C.) was that of the "stone bowl industry" in more southerly parts of New England. Some Archaic bands began to experiment with outcrops of steatite (soapstone), discovering that the stone's softness allowed it to be easily worked into bowls, kettles, cups, ladles, plates and platters. Steatite vessels were sometimes used for cooking (some recovered specimens show burned bottoms) and brought ease

As the more modern deciduous forest continued to spread northward, replacing the predominantly evergreen flora of the earlier Paleo-Indian period, Archaic people found ways to make the new forest's roots, nuts, and seeds more digestible. At first, they ground them with natural cobbles. By the middle of the period, they were using

to food preparation and serving. New culinary creations, such as soups and stews, now supplemented the older fare of meat and fish.

The pitted stone anvil (right) was used to crack tasty nuts offered by the spreading deciduous forest. A bit later in the period, Archaic people began to use the stone mortar and pestle (left) to grind seeds and nuts.

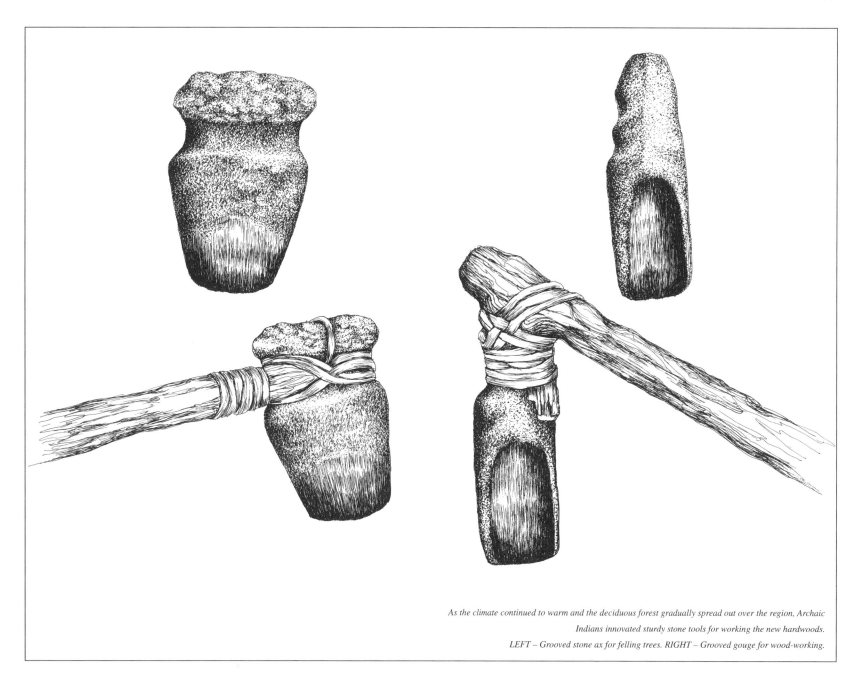

As the climate continued to warm and the deciduous forest gradually spread out over the region, Archaic Indians innovated sturdy stone tools for working the new hardwoods.
LEFT – Grooved stone ax for felling trees. RIGHT – Grooved gouge for wood-working.

The stone ax and gouge were used in the crafting of canoes made from hollowed-out tree trunks. Such watercraft, during this increasingly river-oriented period, became an important means of reaching inland hunting and camping areas and other riverine sites.

28

Even more importantly, these vessels allowed for storage of the wild seeds and nuts that Archaic people had come to rely on as part of their diet: "As people settled into the New England environment and became more adept at (using) all of its food resources, the need for food storage increased...(stone vessels) enabled them to store foods...resulting in an increased ability to cope with seasonal shortages (Hoffman: 78)."

Between 1,700 and 700 B.C., stone bowl making was an important Archaic industry in southeastern New England (where most of the steatite quarry sites seem to have been located). The presence of stone bowl fragments at more northern late Archaic sites – very far from steatite sources – suggests that inter-band trade in products, sometimes over significant distances, did take place in Archaic New England, at least toward the later part of the period.

Important late Archaic quarry sites have been discovered in Providence, Rhode Island; Oaklawn (Cranston), Rhode Island; and Milbury, Massachusetts.

> Work at the quarry was a family affair. Young and old would take the trek to the quarry. Temporary lean-tos were raised against the rock face. Cooking took place at one end of the shelter, while sleeping areas were little more than a handy rock recess. Women and children pitched in to remove the quarry tailings or wastes so that the men could seek out deeper veins of steatite.... Likely, the triangular tailing breaker (a stone quarrying tool) was useful. The women also carried the roughed-out soapstone blanks back to the home site. There the craftsmen could refine them (into stone vessels) at his leisure.
>
> Wilbur: 13

ARCHAIC RELIGION

The full color and texture of Archaic religion, especially for the early part of the period, are heavily obscured by the mists of vast antiquity. Spiritual beliefs and practices perhaps underwent various changes during 6,500 years of Archaic New England life. New Indian bands may have periodically moved into the region from other parts of the country and may have brought new cultural traits that combined with the older traditions. On the basis of excavated stone ceremonial objects and apparent burial customs (to be further discussed in a moment), it is clear that Archaic New Englanders were a deeply spiritual people whose dependence on the natural world fostered a deep reverence for nature and a profound devotion to the perceived deities controlling it.

To insure divine favor and a continued bounty of the landscape's diverse resources, Archaic New Englanders undoubtedly utilized ritual in an attempt to favorably influence the numerous divine beings that were perceived to be at the heart of every single natural object and process (perhaps, as suggested by much later religious traditions in the region, Archaic New Englanders believed that these countless minor deities fell under the dominion of a single Supreme Deity). Since these people occupied New England three thousand years ago and earlier, it is impossible to know anything very specific about their religious rites and world view, although we can make certain assumptions based on ethnographic comparison with other similar hunter-gatherer cultures, as well as by studying the much later and better-known religious customs of New England's Woodland Indians, whose practices were perhaps influenced, at least in part, by those of their much earlier Archaic ancestors. On this basis, it seems reasonable to conclude that:

The Archaic Indian (believed) that his windfalls and downfalls were controlled by the spirits. What else but a displeased spirit could throw down lightning bolts, growl with thunder, and howl in the winds? And when pleased, supply a bounty of game or fish to the hungry? There was no want of these unseen forces. They were everywhere – in the smallest stone or animal to the largest mountain or tree.

To have the best of both worlds – the here and here-after – a prudent Indian must respect the spirit world. He must show honor and pay homage to the kindly spirits or surely fall victim to the merciless powers of the evil ones. Disgrace, illness, or death could be his lot. He needed someone in tune with the spirits to intercede for him – to bring him into their good graces and to drive out the evil powers that tortured him. The shaman, or medicine man, assumed this duty with enthusiasm. If his rituals and techniques were strange to the bedeviled, they were pleasing to the powers he addressed. Only through this middleman could all be made right again. Religion hasn't changed all that much....

Wilbur: 23

Some Late Archaic sites have yielded carved stone effigies – in the shapes of animals, fish, and humans – which were possibly utilized as ritualistic props by shamans. Such effigies – in some cases exquisitely carved – are, in New England, quite rare compared to other types of surviving stone artifacts, suggesting that their use may have been limited to religious rites conducted by medicine men.

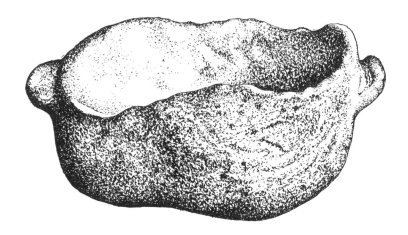

Above: This large soapstone bowl and food serving platter – circa 1500 B.C. – were products of the steatite Stone Bowl Industry in Late Archaic southern New England.

Artifactual remains associated with burials suggest that New England's Archaic people had a pronounced belief in an afterlife. Grave excavations frequently yield numerous stone tools and weapons, whose clear utilitarian design suggests that they were not merely included in graves as tribute, but also to facilitate, for the deceased, the difficult journey into the next world.

Interestingly, some later Archaic graves in New England, especially those of the northern "Maritime Archaic" bands who occupied Maine and areas as far north as the Canadian Provinces between 4,000 and 1,000 B.C., contain profuse amounts of "red ochre," a ground hematite – brilliant red in color – that may have served as some type of funerary ritual paint for the deceased's body (hence, Indians of the northern Maritime Archaic were once called "The Red Paint People" by some archaeologists, although the funerary use of red ochre was not exclusively limited to northern New England). Some archaeologists have suggested that the inclusion of this red paint in Archaic burials had a symbolic ritualistic association with belief in "new" life after death, since red is the color of life-sustaining blood.

CONCLUSIONS

The Archaic period serves to illustrate the effective manner in which New England's Native people continuously fine-tuned their balance with the natural world around them. As the tundra and associated large Pleistocene game animals had disappeared, Archaic Indians progressively developed fresh survival strategies oriented toward the new and gradually stabilizing resources of a warming climate and its associated changes in flora and fauna. The days of pri-

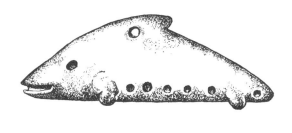

Stone effigies, all from southern Massachusetts. These items may have been used by late Archaic shamans in Native New England rituals that took place more than three thousand years ago.

mary reliance on wandering large game herds were over; New England's Indians now began to adapt themselves to the newly emerging forest of oak and other deciduous species, learning to utilize its seasonal bounties of roots, nuts, and berries, and developing technologies for hunting the new and more diverse animal species that gradually grew in population both on land and in the sea.

As we have seen, the Archaic period was, in general, one of increasingly structured settlement patterns involving, within their respective territories, the seasonally cyclical movements of various Indian bands and, in some parts of the region, eventual gatherings at semi-permanent base camps that were oriented toward spring fish runs that had become reliable annual events. Still, compared to later Indian culture in New England, the Archaic period seems to have been a relatively simple time of fairly small, autonomous bands. Advanced political structuring, social stratification, and perhaps even warfare were likely not components of Archaic Indian culture in New England and would not distinctly emerge until the advent of agriculture and tribal formation during the subsequent Ceramic-Woodland cultural phase, which we will address in Chapter Four.

Many Archaic burials excavated by New England archaeologists contain numerous grave goods such as tools and weapons, which were likely placed in with the deceased for his or her use on the long journey into the next world.

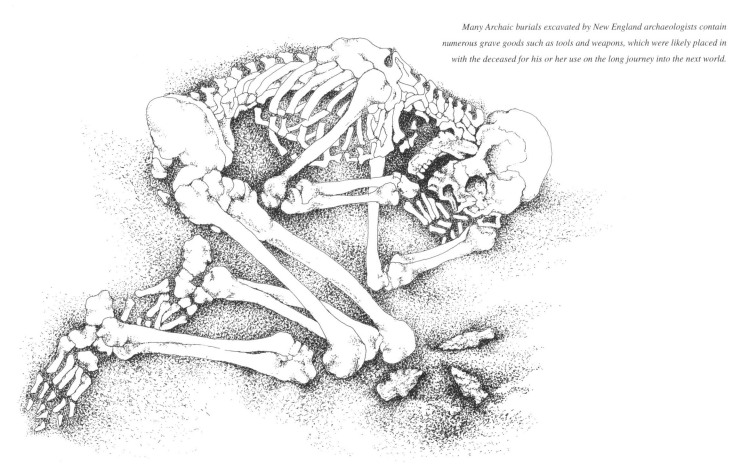

Chapter Three

Archaic Creativity: Two Rare Examples

Part I
A Previously Unpublished Archaic Sweat Lodge

Some 4,500 years ago, a small Late Archaic band of about twenty or thirty Indians began to camp in Rehoboth, Massachusetts, for a good part of the fall, not far from what is today the Rehoboth Village. Evidence suggests that they returned to the same general spot year after year. Their six acre campsite was ideally located on a sandy plateau overlooking a sparkling, spring-fed stream (or, topographical evidence suggests, perhaps even a lake, long since dried up) that provided fresh water. The spot was a pleasant one for the season, with a nice, dry elevation and lush surrounding woods in which the band hunted birds and found flavorful hickory nuts for later roasting by the evening fires. A short walk away was the Palmer River, where the men could launch their canoes and navigate to hunting areas deeper within the forest, while the women and children back at the campsite skinned animal hides with stone scrapers, readying the skins for use as clothing in preparation for the impending winter.

Until fairly recently, this Massachusetts campsite was obscurely hidden away under centuries of wind-deposited soil layers. Aside from an occasional timeworn arrowhead or burned hearth stone making its way to the modern-day surface, the site was a barren, sandy knoll that gave little indication of its ancient occupation.

Yet, the human activities that took place on this spot several millennia ago have become discernible. Through careful archaeological excavation, some of the buried tools, weapons, and even foodstuffs of this small Archaic band have once again seen the light of day. Under analysis, these fragments of New England prehistory have also revealed evidence of an enigmatic underground chamber – what seems to have been a sauna-like sweat lodge – which represents an unprecedented discovery for an Archaic New England site (the much later Woodland Indians were known to have used sweat lodges; thus, for the first time, we have evidence of an earlier Archaic origin for this fascinating tradition).

Beginning in 1986, the Cohannet Chapter of the Massachusetts Archaeological Society initiated controlled excavations of the site, under the direction of Brady Fitts. At this time, the site was formally named the Tobey Site, after the property owners.

Excavations continued periodically for the next five years. Eventually, Fitts and his team of researchers uncovered numerous stone artifacts and site features. Carbon-dating of associated charcoal indicated that the Archaic occupation of this ancient site began at least as early as 2,700 B.C.

Evidence suggests that the site was likely used for fall encampments. The discovery of traces of charred hickory nuts and bird bones points to occupations in fall, when these foods would have been plentiful, while the complete absence of fish bone seems to preclude spring or summer occupations. Additionally, stone fire hearths (for warmth as well as for cooking) were too few in number to suggest occupations during winter. Thus, the site was probably used, perhaps year after year, as an autumn stopover by a small band of Archaic Indians who may have left some larger seasonal summer fishing camp with the coming of fall (perhaps the nearby Wampanucket #6 site at Assowompsett Lake in Middleboro, Massachusetts, which falls within the same general time frame) and who were on their way to winter hunting grounds farther inland, where small winter game was most prevalent – away from the cold winter winds of the seaside.

Fitts and his assistants excavated the site using a grid layout system. After some sixty squares (each one a square meter in size) had been opened, a number of notable features came to light. For instance, three cooking hearths were unearthed; these were roughly circular arrangements of stones (found disturbed and somewhat scattered, probably by frost action) that contained charcoal and other evidence of fires. As noted above, researchers also found nearby traces of charred hickory nuts and bird bones, indicating that the camp's occupants had sat around the hearths roasting these foods.

At another section of the site, excavators unearthed a high concentration of stone scraping tools. It seems that this section of the camp was a specialized workshop area for skinning animal hides (based on ethnographic comparison with similar groups, this was probably a task performed by the women and children of the band, while men and young boys were undoubtedly responsible for hunting). Once scraped clean, the hides were subsequently used for clothing and for shelter covering (shelters at the campsite consisted

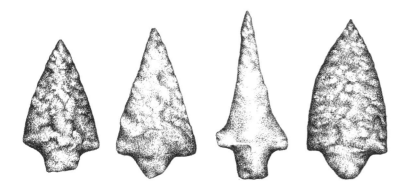

Stone projectile points and drill specimens, circa 2,700 B.C., recovered from the Tobey Site in Rehoboth, Massachusetts.

of brush or sapling frameworks, over which animal skins were stretched for protection against the elements). At least thirty stone hide scrapers were found in this part of the camp.

At other sections of the site, Fitts and his team recovered numerous projectile points, a sharpening stone, a crude plummet, and stone anvils for cracking nuts. In total, over 1,000 stone artifacts were unearthed. With this site, as with so many others, one might ask why so many belongings were left behind after the band departed. One likely explanation is that Archaic groups, during times of seasonal mobility, did not wish to carry heavy loads. When leaving a particular site, Indians left certain items behind, since it was probably easier to craft new ones at the next encampment, rather than transport everything from one site to the next. Additionally, artifacts may have been intentionally stored or buried for future use during a prospective return visit and, for one reason or another, these caches were never recovered.

Perhaps the most striking discovery made at the Tobey Site was the unearthing of what seems to have been a sweat lodge – a partially subterranean enclosure that the camp's inhabitants may have utilized as a sort of heated "sauna" – to cleanse the skin and perhaps also for certain types of purification rituals. Fitts and his research team describe finding the remains of a circular structure, about fourteen feet in diameter and with a small entrance, which had been built partially underground. The above-ground portion of the structure had likely consisted of a sapling frame roof covered with mud and leaves. At the center of the underground portion of the enclosure, excavators found a scooped-out fire pit, which may have been used to illuminate the interior of the structure and/or to hold a smudge fire for repelling mosquitoes. Fitts and his team also discovered a small earth platform or "seat" near this central fireplace, which was apparently occupied by the person who tended the fire.

Immediately adjacent to the remains of the structure were a large number of burned stones, which, it seems, were heated outside and were then brought into the structure to warm it to a suitable level for "sweating." Once the stones were inside, the occupants of the lodge probably threw water on them to generate steam.

Later colonial accounts of Woodland Indian sweat lodges in New England give us some idea of how this earlier Archaic example may have been utilized. One colonial observer noted the following:

> They were made as a vault, partly underground, and in the form of a large oven, where two or three persons might on occasion sit together, and their method was to heat stones very hot in the fire, and put them into the

(sweat lodge), and when the persons were in, to shut it close up with only so much air as was necessary for respiration...and being thus closely pent up, the heat of the stones occasioned them to sweat in a prodigious manner, streaming as it were from every part of their bodies, and when they had continued there for as long as they could well endure it, their method was to rush out and plunge themselves into (some nearby) water. By this means they (seek) a cure of all pains and numbness in their joints and many other maladies.

Samuel Niles (1760)

Archaeologists' computerized field view, in overview perspective, of the Tobey Site:
A) Cooking hearths; B) Remnants of charred hickory nuts and bird bones; C) Charred hickory nuts; D) Sweat lodge; E) Stones once used to heat sweat lodge; F) Concentration of stone scrapers – part of camp once used for working animal hides.

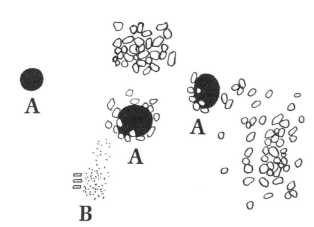

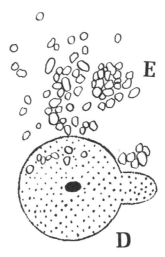

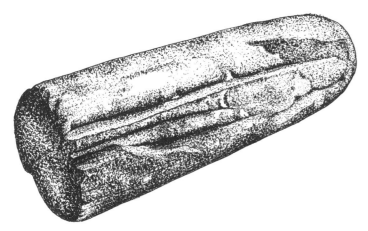

Sharpening stone found at the Tobey Site. Channeled grooves were left by the repeated sharpening of bone awls and other tools along the stone's surface.

Roger Williams has also left us with an account of Indian sweat lodges in early colonial New England:

...they had exceedingly heated it with a store of wood, laid upon an heape of stones in the middle. When they had taken out the fire, the stones keep still a great heat...(the men) enter at once starke naked...here do they sit around their hot stones an houre or more... discoursing and sweating together; which sweating they use for two ends: First to cleanse their skin: Secondly to purge their bodies, which doubtless is a great means of preserving them, and recovering them from diseases....

Williams (1643)

While the Tobey Site sweat lodge dates to a much earlier period (a radio-carbon date of charcoal taken from the lodge dates the structure to about 2,700 B.C.), its general construction suggests that it was probably utilized in very much the same manner as the later structures described in the above accounts. What these colonial writers were probably observing, then, was the continuation of an

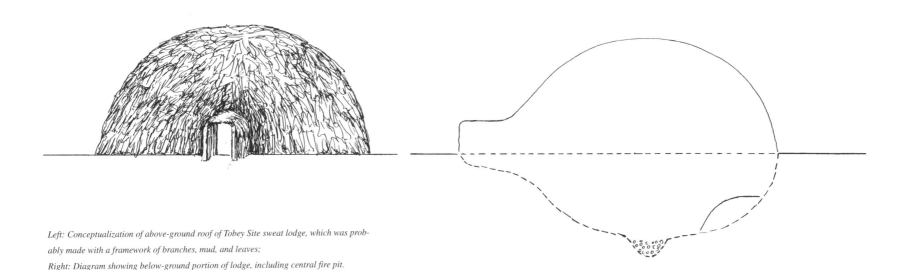

Left: Conceptualization of above-ground roof of Tobey Site sweat lodge, which was probably made with a framework of branches, mud, and leaves;
Right: Diagram showing below-ground portion of lodge, including central fire pit.

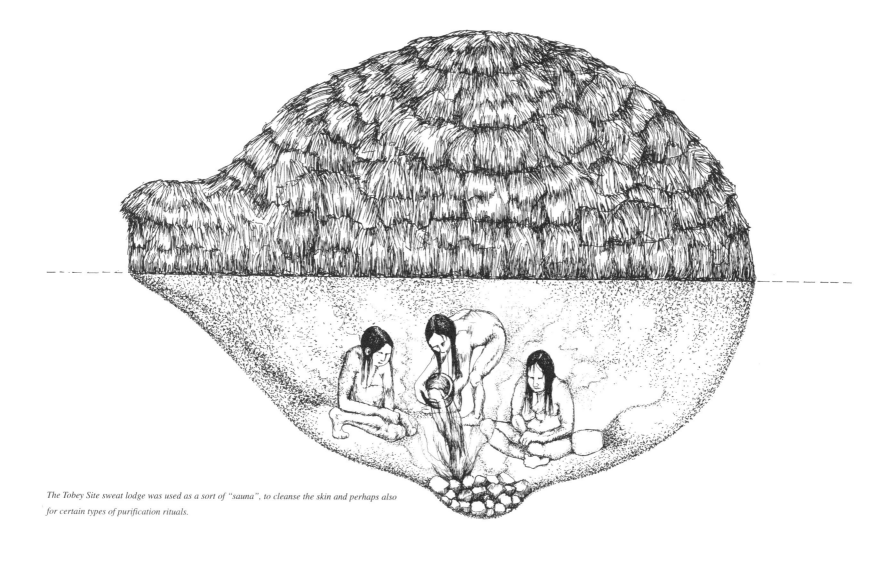

The Tobey Site sweat lodge was used as a sort of "sauna", to cleanse the skin and perhaps also for certain types of purification rituals.

ancient tradition that dated back to the much earlier Archaic period, as suggested by the presence of the sweat lodge at Rehoboth's Tobey Site. Such a finding at an Archaic site is unique in New England, and it attests to the creativity of an Archaic people who apparently knew how to live life well.

Part II

The "Boat Site" – Creative Archaic Funerary Rites

The Boat Site, which lies on the west bank of the Taunton River in Dighton, Massachusetts, was excavated, in the 1950's, by a researcher named Howard Rose. Because of its ideal location on this major river, the site was apparently used over many centuries by various Indian bands. Occupations began at least as early as the early Archaic and continued over the next several thousand years. For almost a century prior to Rose's excavation, artifact hunters had been removing vast quantities of antiquities that had been upturned by plowing. Unfortunately, such an extensive amount of artifact hunting meant that much valuable archaeological evidence had already been removed from the site before Rose's controlled excavation was initiated.

While a detailed picture of the campsite cannot be inferred from the disturbed and fragmentary remains left by pothunters, a few components of the site were spared destruction. Most notably, Rose documented a series of late Archaic burials at the site, and these graves have yielded some sparse but intriguing information concerning the funerary rites of these very ancient New England inhabitants.

The graves appeared as circular pits, averaging from fifteen to thirty inches in diameter and about eight to ten inches in depth. Bits of charcoal and bone appearing in the pits suggest that these early Indians practiced cremation. Each pit probably contained the remains of a single individual. Interestingly, some of the pits also contained red ochre, bright red hematite that had been ground into a fine powder and had apparently then been sprinkled in with the human remains. As indicated earlier, such a practice was perhaps associated with some notion of an afterlife. Because red hematite resembles the color of life-sustaining blood, these Archaic people

may have thought that the substance was infused with some sort of magical, life-giving property. Thus, it was perhaps believed that the red ochre, when sprinkled on the remains of the deceased, turned into blood, thereby allowing life to continue beyond the grave.

The mourners had also placed a variety of stone implements in the cremation pits, again suggestive of a belief in continued existence beyond death. So that the deceased would be prepared for the difficult journey into the next world, he or she was provided with such items as stone knives, projectile points, and drills. The aesthetic quality of these grave goods was superb, seemingly better than would be expected for regular items made for normal, daily use. In the same manner that we select the finest gravestones possible for loved ones we have lost – since this is the last thing we will ever be able to do for them – these Indians seem to have sent off their deceased with the best burial goods they could provide, as a creative final gesture of their love and devotion.

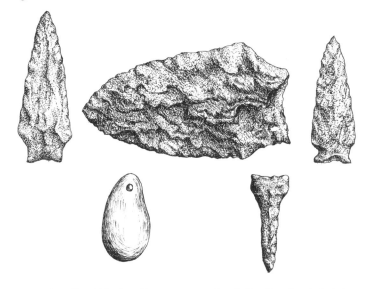

Carefully wrought and beautifully shaped in stone, grave goods at the Boat Site reflect the Archaic stoneworker's creativity and talent.

Chapter Four

The Ceramic-Woodland Indian Period
500 B.C. to 1600 A.D.

OVERVIEW

By 500 B.C., some northeastern Indian bands, in addition to trading among themselves, had established long-distance trading relationships with Indian groups well to the west of the region – most notably, Adena Indian villagers living in the Ohio Valley area. The Adena were a textured and colorful people known for their post and wattle houses, settled villages, pottery, and use of Great Lakes copper for tools and ornaments. Most importantly, the Adena grew food crops, including squash, gourds, and, eventually, maize/corn (the practice of farming had originated farther south during the Archaic period – among Indian groups living in what are now Mexico and Peru – and had slowly diffused across the Americas, reaching the Adena and other people in the Ohio River Valley area by the later part of the Archaic period, when New England's Indians were still entirely dependent on hunting and gathering).

By the end of the Archaic period, northeastern Indian groups living in New York and Vermont were sending small trading expeditions to the Ohio Valley; exactly what goods these northeastern traders offered the western Adena is uncertain, though we know that they brought back copper and seashell ornaments, fancy weights and pipes, stone pendants, and beautifully carved and polished stone objects shaped like birds, often called "birdstones." Once back from the Ohio Valley, the traders exchanged these western-derived Adena objects with their nearby neighbors in different parts of New England, explaining why Adena objects from the Ohio Valley are occasionally found in New England archaeological deposits of the period.

Via these long-distance trade routes, Adena influence on New England's various Indian bands was, in time, wholly transformative, for it seems that the traders brought more than Adena goods and objects back to New England. From about 500 B.C. onward, they also carried back certain western ideas, customs, and technologies, all of which would gradually spread through the region and, although it would take many years, would profoundly alter the lives of New England's inhabitants.

Pottery-making was the first new technology to gradually diffuse over the region, eventually supplanting stone bowl manufacture as a cultural focal point. Then, about 500 A.D., long-distance trade with the west brought the bow and arrow to New England. Later in the period, by about 1000 A.D. and perhaps even earlier, Indian groups

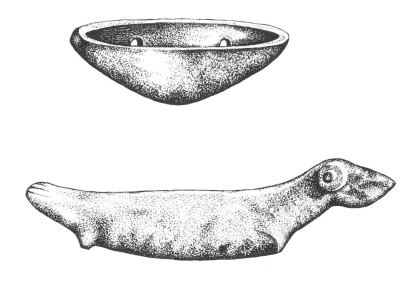

Adena "boat-stone" (top) and "bird-stone" (bottom). These enigmatic artifacts – whose use is unknown – filtered into New England via long-distance trade routes with the west.

in some parts of New England began to adopt Adena-style subsistence strategies, most notably that of corn cultivation, which allowed for an increasingly stable and storable food supply. This development eventually resulted in larger local populations; the emergence, in some areas, of sizable agricultural villages; the eventual grouping of some of these villages into large, culturally distinct tribes; a more settled (though not entirely sedentary) existence; and, finally, the development of increasingly complex social and political structures.

This later phase of Ceramic-Woodland culture represents the one that was encountered by 17th-century white colonists, some of whom have left us with textured written accounts (often biased, but descriptive nonetheless) of aboriginal life and customs. Therefore, while our knowledge of Archaic and, especially, earlier Paleo-Indian culture remains extremely fragmentary, information concerning this later period is relatively substantive. Hence, this chapter – in its examination of Indian customs and beliefs – is significantly more detailed and colorful than those preceding it (for an even more detailed discussion of certain important Ceramic-Woodland customs – such as cooking, legends, and medicinals – the reader is directed to the appendix section of this book).

SETTLEMENT PATTERNS

At first, with the exception of the gradual spread of pottery manufacture and use, life in the early part of the Ceramic-Woodland period was, for most of the various Indian bands living in different parts of New England, a continuation of the hunting-gathering patterns of the preceding Archaic culture. Within their respective territories, bands continued to move in seasonally cyclical patterns dependent on the annual availability of diverse natural resources, with some bands spending a good part of each year at their favorite fair-weather base camps.

As time progressed, more and more bands adopted the use of pottery, and, eventually, most New England Indians were using ceramic vessels for all of their cooking and for the storage of foods. Food storage, though sometimes practiced in the Archaic period with stone vessels, seems to have become even more common by the beginning of the Ceramic-Woodland period, indicating that various bands had become even more strategically adapted to the New England environment. Ceramic vessels – filled with nuts, seeds, and dried berries – were placed in the ground, in large storage pits, during the summer and fall, allowing people to get through the hard winter months more easily than before – although this was a far cry from the extensive food storage that would soon be permitted by agriculture.

At the beginning and for quite a few years, then, the Ceramic-Woodland period was, with the exception of certain changes like pottery and the increased use of food storage pits, in many ways similar to the preceding Archaic period. However, as noted earlier, new ideas from the Ohio Valley had been filtering into the region via trade routes. When one of them – agriculture – began to take hold in New England about 1000 A.D., regional culture would dramatically change:

Above: Very plain and simple at first, the pottery of prehistoric New England eventually featured exquisite form and design.

When the Indians learned how to plant and raise maize, a major change took place in their way of life. Agricultural skills made it possible to lay up a store of food for the winter to an extent not possible before...the day of hand-to-mouth living was over. Of course, they continued to hunt and fish – berries and nuts were still part of their diet – but the day of complete dependence of natural foods was gone. However, the very existence of these new sources of grown food would tie them to the land. They could no longer roam the way they had in the old days; during the spring and summer the growing crop must be protected from predators. After the harvest was gathered and the grain stored in pits, they had to stay close by the stores...primitive transportation means were not adequate to permit quantities of stores to be moved far. But population increased as the ability to support life increased: villages grew larger. There was also another aspect of the stable economy. No longer was all of the aborigine's time taken up by the everlasting quest for food. There were leisure moments in which one could begin to think about better ways of life. Social and political ideas began to form and ceremonial concepts further developed. This significant change in subsistence pattern not only forced the Indians to forsake nomadism, but it encouraged them to recognize the non-material traits which mark a step along the road to civilization. These cultural changes are most apparent in the archaeological recoveries from Woodland villages.

Robbins 1969: 11

Between 1000 and 1500 A.D., earlier settlement patterns involving relatively small and dispersed groups were, in many (though not all) parts of New England, gradually replaced by larger settlements centered around agriculture. Populations increased, and strong iden-

tities grew up around these growing horticultural villages and their geographical locations, resulting in the eventual emergence of geographically distinct tribes (tribes perhaps resulted when, in a particular territory, several agricultural villages banded together to protect their crops and fertile soils from outside intrusion. These banded settlements not only thought of their territory as uniquely their own, but, in time, also developed customs and beliefs unique to them – resulting in a distinct tribal identity).

Because New England's prehistoric people left no written records, we do not know exactly how particular tribes evolved. Agriculture and associated tribal development took hold at different times in various parts of New England – in some areas sooner, in others quite a bit later. Tribes were in many ways culturally similar because of common earlier origins; all were of the same blood and spoke the same Eastern Algonquin language (although differences in dialect evolved from tribe to tribe). But each tribe would come to have its own rulers and, as noted, lands that it considered its own.

For instance, the populous Rhode Island Narragansett Tribe organized itself around the shores and islands of Narragansett Bay (with the exception of the Mount Hope section to the east). The Massachusetts Tribe, a numerous people, became centralized around southern Massachusetts Bay and Boston Harbor, and southeastern Massachusetts became home to the Wampanoag Tribe. Eastern Connecticut eventually belonged to the powerful Pequots and their subject Mohegans. New Hampshire became home to the Pennacooks. A portion of Maine fell under dominion of the Abenaki Tribe (this last group was a hunting people, since its territory was too cold for planting).

The above listing is a mere sampling; there were numerous other minor tribes in various parts of New England. All, except the north-eastern-most of New England's Indians, became, at least in part,

Agriculture brought increased stability to the food supply.
Stone and clamshell hoes were hafted to long wooden handles.

42

agricultural people sooner or later – with a few exceptions (in some upland and inland areas far from the coast, as well as in extreme northern areas too cold for agriculture, there apparently remained some groups who continued, even in the later part of the period, to maintain the non-agricultural hunting-gathering patterns of earlier times).

Each tribe's territory was usually well-defined; its boundaries were designated by such natural landscape features as drainage basins, hills, streams and other physical limits that were traditionally recognized – and taken very seriously – by other tribal groups. If a tribe chose to infringe on the territorial hunting or planting grounds of another – even if the encroachment was casual – hostility and even warfare could ensue. A single tribe's territory was often vast (the exact size and quality varied from tribe to tribe, depending on the group's strength and location); ideally, it contained enough lands for village sites, fields for cultivation, a good fishing site, and good hunting grounds (agriculture had by no means precluded the hunt; animal proteins were especially essential in winter). Within its territory, a tribe often maintained several separate though interactive villages, all of which fell under the authority of a single tribal chief (sachem) and each of which might be headed by a subordinate chief (or sagamore).

Main tribal villages were customarily located at coastal or major riverine valley sites, where the soil was most fertile for planting corn, beans, and squash:

> Tribes preferred a physically attractive spot for settlement. Almost without exception the sites chosen for villages combined a number of advantages: an elevation with a pleasing view, yet defensible; protection from the north wind by a hill or a thicket of evergreens; a clear,

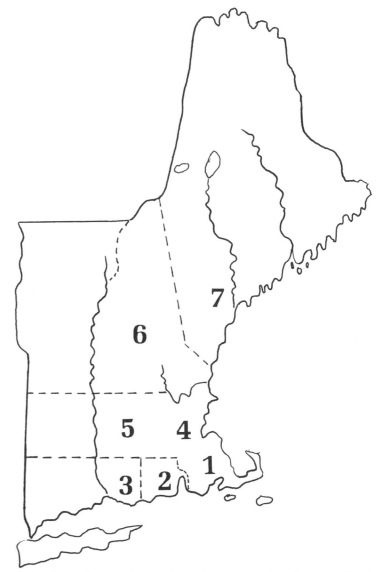

Some major New England tribes and their territorial centers (note: numerous minor tribes are not indicated): 1 – Wampanoags. 2 – Narragansetts. 3 – Pequots and Mohegans. 4 Massachusetts. 5 – Nipmucs. 6 – Pennacooks. 7 – Abenakis.

flowing spring; and a source of firewood nearby. The site would be close to the sea; to one or more lakes, where fishing was good; to a large river (preferably the confluence of two streams); or, better still, all three...the waters would offer ease of canoe transportation as well as food...the inhabitants would probably not stay for the whole year at the new village site. They would very likely spend a few weeks at the seashore or at a great waterfall, seeking fish to cure – and also to enjoy pleasant company, games, and contests.

Russell: 51

Somewhere near the village site, inhabitants found a pine plain or other "light" land that could be cleared – sometimes using fire to clean out underbrush – to provide fields for crops, as well as clearings for nut groves, berry fields, and deer-attracting pastures. Larger villages were probably occupied for a good part of each year, though village life was not completely sedentary. While some villagers (perhaps the elderly, for instance) may have stayed in the main villages virtually year-round, most seem to have moved between the main village and smaller, seasonal campsites.

Specific patterns of movement varied in different parts of the region; in many parts of New England, during the spring and summer, inhabitants sometimes left the crops to mature (perhaps leaving a small group behind to guard the fields), departing the village for a few weeks in order to spend some time at a favorite coastal gathering spot or great waterfall, as noted earlier, where they could catch fish (which they smoked for later transport back to the village) and interact with Indians from other villages or tribes. Additionally, after the fall harvest, village inhabitants in many parts of the region (including all of southern New England) often departed the village and temporarily relocated to inland campsites and hunting grounds, where they spent the winter in game areas that were better protected from

icy winds. As spring approached, they returned to the main village and began the planting cycle all over again. In time, when the soil became spent from repeated cultivation, the entire village would be relocated to a fresh, more fertile site.

LIFE IN THE VILLAGE

Marriage and the nuclear family were important facets of Ceramic-Woodland tribal life. Within villages, each family often had its own private dwelling, though two or more families sometimes shared a larger structure – known as a "longhouse" – that was divided into sections in which each family had its own hearth and living quarters. Individual family dwellings were snug and secure. In southern New England villages, they were known as "wigwams" and consisted of circular sapling frameworks, measuring about six meters across, that were covered with woven mats or bark shingling. A flapped opening on the roof of the structure, which could be closed with the pull of a string, served as a smoke vent and skylight. Family dwellings in northern New England villages were somewhat similar, though sometimes they were much more conical in appearance. Multiple-family longhouses appeared in both northern and southern New England villages.

Each dwelling contained a fire hearth, comfortable beds of woven mats and animal furs, and the family's various household equipment, which might include ceramic cooking pots, a small stone mortar and pestle for grinding foods, a few storage baskets left hanging from the rafters, some wooden plates, and various stone tools and utensils. Sometimes, women decorated the inside wall of the family wigwam with embroidered and dyed hangings. In some cases, families shared their wigwams with one or more domesticated dogs, though these animals were not really "pets" in the true sense of the word (rather, this intelligent, wolf-derived breed was used for hunting and for keeping the village grounds free of garbage and rodents. Sometimes,

An agricultural village. Wooden stockades may have enclosed the village during times of war, though they were probably not common.

when game was scarce, dogs may have used as a reserve food supply).

Family dwellings were usually clustered around a large, central open area in the village. Here, villagers could gather for ceremonial, political, and recreational activities. In addition to individual dwellings, villages often contained larger ceremonial lodges in which secret, mystical religious rites were conducted. These lodges were the domain of the shaman – the medicine man – and were probably strictly off-limits to the general populace except at certain designated times.

In cases where villagers perceived a threat from a rival tribe, they could opt to enclose the village with a protective wooden stockade. Such enclosures seem to have been rare in New England, however; in general, as people who cherished nature and savored the beauty and vastness of the surrounding landscape, New England's Indians were not – perhaps with the exception of cases in which a known rival was about to attack – inclined to close themselves in (in fact, when they first observed the homes of white colonial settlers many years later, the Algonquin tribes were perplexed. Why, they wondered, would the white man want to voluntarily jail himself by constructing a house and choosing to spend so much time within its dark, enclosed confines?)

Over time, as populations grew, villages also increased in size; some tribes maintained only a few simple villages with relatively small populations, but, as the period progressed, an occasional tribal village might have eventually accommodated as many as a few hundred people (the tribe itself, in some instances, eventually included as many as a few thousand people, living in many separate villages – connected by footpaths and rivers – within the same general territory). Such exceptionally large villages, rare as they were at this size level, grew, in the later part of the period, into bustling places: "Life

in a very large village was probably noisy, smoky, busy...after all, these were really small towns, with many people and even more dogs. Imagine the sounds and smells of such a busy place!" (Brown : 76)

In general, however, the agricultural villages of New England's various tribes were, for the most part, dispersed and quite modest and were still supplemented with smaller seasonal campsites. Villages were nothing like the elaborate "cities" of prehistoric people – like the Anasazi or Maya – in certain other parts of the country. With the stabilization afforded by agriculture, New England Indian culture, had it been left to itself to further adapt and evolve, would have been gradually on its way to an increasingly elaborate village system – with more and larger villages and increasingly sophisticated wooden (and, eventually, perhaps even stone) structures. However, the interruption of New England culture by white settlers only several hundred years after agriculture and its attendant cultural benefits had begun to take hold would thwart any chances for further advance and development, as we shall see in the following chapter.

POLITICAL AND SOCIAL LIFE

As noted earlier, the advent of agriculture had resulted in more leisure time for the contemplation of relatively sophisticated political concepts. The emergence of distinct and often large tribal groupings had brought with it progressive societal structuring. The simple, egalitarian ways of earlier times were now gone, having been gradually replaced by the evolution of well-defined social hierarchies within most tribes:

A chief sachem governed each tribe, and subordinate sachems or sagamores headed its various divisions or villages.... In southern New England, the chieftainship was usually hereditary, descending through the mother, per-

The wigwam, a single-family dwelling typical of villages throughout southern New England.

Interior of family wigwam.

haps to a sister's offspring.... In some northern New England tribes, however, the new chief's influence would depend to a greater extent on his own character, abilities, and prestige.

However high a chief's standing, he had a lively regard for public opinion: he seldom exercised his authority in important matters without a careful canvass of his council – chosen for their wisdom and ability – and his subordinate sachems.

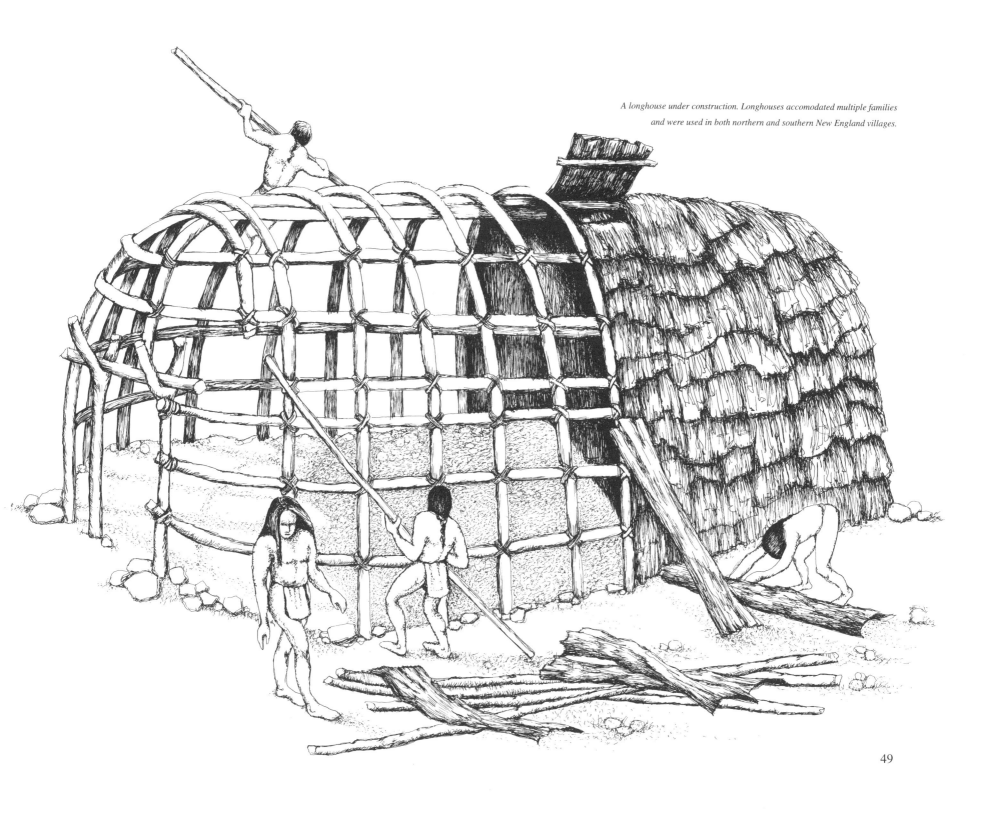

A longhouse under construction. Longhouses accomodated multiple families and were used in both northern and southern New England villages.

49

Interior of a longhouse.

The elderly were held in honor. Where weighty themes were considered, the members of the council of elders and subchiefs as well were called into consultation. The conclave might include women, for they were the food producers and persons of experience and good judgment. In several instances, women of high birth headed New England Indian groups as sachems. Sometimes as widows they succeeded their husbands; others were chosen when an able male of the princely line was lacking.

Russell: 19-20

Most tribes became socially stratified. Subordinates to the sachem usually fell into one of three categories: 1) nobles of superior blood (perhaps related to the royal family of the sachem) or persons of important religious or military achievement, 2) commoners, called "sannops," who made up the bulk of the tribe as a sort of "middle class," or 3) "outsiders" – stray or captured persons who were adopted into the tribe (often as servants) and who had few legal rights within the tribal community.

As for material and resource ownership, it had both private and communal aspects, though primarily the latter. Tools, ornaments, weapons, food, and clothing were personal property (subject, at times, to the hospitality or sharing customs of the tribe). Each family was given its own plot of land for the cultivation of crops, though some planting fields were collectively worked. Hunting grounds and wood sources were communally shared by all families. The sachem usually controlled the use of territorial lakes and streams.

ROLES OF THE SEXES, SEXUALITY, MARRIAGE, AND CHILDREN

Within each tribe, there were well-defined divisions of labor between the sexes. Upon cursory review, one might assume that these divisions were unfairly balanced, for while men spent much of their time hunting and fishing, women were generally responsible for making pottery, planting and tending to the crops, maintaining the household, caring for infants, preparing meals, gathering firewood, collecting nuts and berries, and weaving clothing and baskets. However, it would be a mistake to conclude that the women's world was one of pure drudgery and the men's one of relative ease. Contrary to certain later colonial accounts, hunting was not necessarily light work for the men, who had to pursue and capture sufficient amounts of game and fish to keep their families well-supplied with animal proteins, especially in fall and winter. The hunt was not a "sport;" rather, it was arduous and often exhausting. Tracking and running down a single deer or moose could take an entire day, and then the heavy beast, or parts thereof, had to be carried back to the settlement, sometimes over great distances.

Additionally, men were responsible for making tools and weapons, crafting dugout and birch-bark canoes, felling trees when

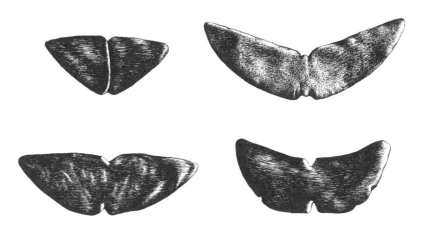

These enigmatic artifacts, known as "whale-tail" pendants, may have been worn as a badge of office as tribes became socially stratified. Their precise function is not certain, however.

Although women were responsible for such tasks as harvesting and grinding the corn, as seen here, they often played an important role in tribal decision-making.

52

clearings were needed, and, when necessary, for waging war and engaging in trade and diplomatic interaction with other tribes.

While Indian women were clearly responsible for a variety of demanding tasks, their importance in tribal life far transcended that of mere industry. As noted previously, women sometimes served as sachems. Even where the tribal chief was male – which was most often the case – women frequently played a significant role in councils and community decision-making. Thus, to an extent unusual for such an early culture, women seem to have been afforded a high degree of respect and equality; their talents, abilities, and intelligence were acknowledged, and they were not culturally conditioned into a fully submissive orientation:

> As a person, a woman was the unquestioned mistress of her body. If unmarried, she might without shame accept a bed companion or withhold her favor as she preferred. Unmarried pregnancy was, however, a disgrace – to be avoided, if necessary, by the use of plant preventatives. Violation of the chastity of unconsenting girls is said to have been unknown, as was the rape or abuse of a married woman. Incest incurred disgrace.
>
> Russell: 97

In marriage, monogamy was generally the rule, although a chief or shaman sometimes had several wives in addition to his primary spouse. Marriage required parental approval, and a dowry was requested of the bride's family. While not common, divorce was socially permissible, whether of the husband's or wife's choosing (women who left their husbands often joined another tribe, bringing their children with them). In most cases, however, marriage bonds were strong. "One husband was known to frequently travel forty miles and back on foot, two days' journey, for cranberries as medicine for his ill wife (Russell: 98)." Widows, though free to remarry, usually did not.

When a woman gave birth, her husband prepared a smooth, flat cradle board onto which the infant could be strapped and carried about on its mother's back. To prevent chafing, the child was wrapped in a fluff-filled covering. The baby was not pampered. Within three days of its birth, it was already being transported about in a little backback, which could be hung on a nearby tree branch if the mother wanted to grind some corn or tend to her crops.

From an early age, children of both sexes were expected to practice and acquire the crafts and skills that would be required of them in adulthood. Young girls helped their mothers to plant, harvest, pick berries, cook, make pottery, and weave baskets, while fathers taught their young sons how to maneuver about in the woods, track and bring down game, fish, and craft weapons. Both girls and boys were continuously instructed in the legends, signals, and religious customs of their tribe. Indian children also had time for play, and archaeologists have found small clay dolls and other objects that undoubtedly served as toys.

INTER-TRIBAL TRADE AND WARFARE

The emergence of separate tribal groupings saw significant inter-territorial trade and, in some instances, conflict. Trade among New England tribes primarily involved ceremonial objects and items of personal adornment, including shell beads (called wampumpeague, the most prized of which were the black ones made by the Rhode Island Narragansetts), steatite and clay pipes (in addition to corn, beans, and squash, some tribes began to grow tobacco, which was primarily used in ritual), and other non-necessity commodities that passed between tribes in barter or peace offerings.

The frequency of warfare between New England tribes is uncertain. When it did occur, it was usually the result of jealousy, insult, or, most often, territorial dispute. The Massachusetts Wampanoags,

The bow and arrow – which was imported into New England from the west early on in the Ceramic-Woodland period – was significantly more accurate than the earlier atlatl stick and was used both in hunting and warfare.

for instance, were at times in conflict with the Rhode Island Narragansetts over issues of tribal territory, though such disputes were usually temporary. When battles did occur, they could range from small skirmishes to full-scale blood baths.

While most New England tribes did not maintain standing armies per se, their sports and games emphasized and fostered warrior prowess. Males improved their strength and agility by participating in tournaments of stickball, wrestling, running, and marksmanship. A male was usually not deemed a ready warrior until about the age of sixteen, at which point he might undergo a test of his courage and manhood. For example, in the dead of winter, the boy's fellow tribesmen might lead him blindfolded into the wilderness, where he would be left to survive alone, armed only with a bow, some arrows, a hatchet, and a knife. In the spring, the boy returned to the village, and his appearance would tell of his success or failure – and his readiness to serve as a warrior.

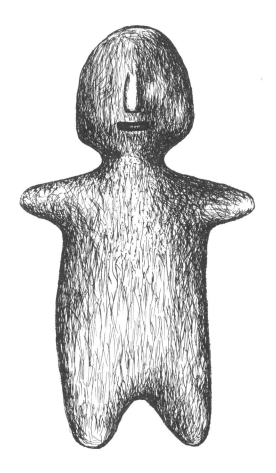

A tiny ceramic doll found at Cape Cod. This was likely the toy of a little Wampanoag girl.

Stone pendants for adornment were common items of inter-tribal trade.

When warfare between two rival tribes seemed imminent, each tribe conducted a solemn war dance ritual in which a war captain (or the tribal sachem himself) recounted the wrongs of the enemy and stirred his tribesmen to battle:

> A drum began its slow pulse-rated beat. The war leader took up his club and smeared it with vermilion to symbolize blood. The measured beat continued, now accompanied by a rattle and the songs of one or more warriors. The leader stamped the ground as if to shake the universe. His dance was highly figurative...involving the influence of the spirits upon him. He sang brief songs of heroic exploits and military deeds that would excite his audience....Every warrior who rose and joined the dance became a volunteer for battle. By so enlisting himself, the warrior could not honorably withdraw.
>
> Wilbur: 49

Indian warfare generally followed certain customs, some of them quite honorable. For instance, an attacking tribe might forewarn its enemy by placing an arrow near the target village, or by forwarding a sheath of arrows via a messenger. Once such a warning had been given, an attack could follow at any time during the ensuing weeks or months, usually at a time least expected. To afford themselves camouflage, and to render their appearance more terrifying, attacking warriors often painted various unsettling designs onto their bodies, including fantastic images of serpents and demons. Then, they stealthily approached the enemy village, usually besieging it at dawn while the inhabitants were still asleep. Additional warriors often hid themselves in the surrounding woods, waiting in ambush for any villagers who might try to flee.

Indian combat could be vicious and bloody. While some warriors employed arrows against their opponents, the bolder combatants often preferred hand to hand fighting in which they could demonstrate their courage and strength to fellow tribesmen. The weapons used in these close encounters were lethal. They included razor-sharp stone hatchets and wooden war clubs studded with deadly stone prongs. Sometimes, warriors wore rawhide shields on their upper torsos to protect the heart from penetrating arrows.

During an attack on an enemy village, the aggressors sometimes took prisoners. Women and children were usually spared and were assimilated into the tribe's lowest "outsider" class. Adult male prisoners were usually not so fortunate. Often they were executed by slow, excruciating torture (actually, this type of death was a courtesy extended to the captured warrior, for it gave him a chance to die with honor by standing firm and not crying out during the ordeal. As word spread that he had endured the torture stoically, his own people and even his captors honored and praised his name, sealing his reputation as a great warrior. To die a quick, painless death – with no chance to demonstrate warrior courage and thereby win honor – would have been the worst way a captured warrior could think of to die). However, not all adult male prisoners were executed. In some cases, a captured warrior became the surrogate husband of a woman whose spouse had fallen in battle.

Archaeological evidence for warfare has been unearthed at several important New England sites. One especially interesting discovery was unearthed at the Titicut Site, a Ceramic-Woodland village site situated by southeastern Massachusetts' extensive Taunton River. Here, in 1947, the Massachusetts Archaeological Society excavated the skull of a young Indian male who had been struck in the head by an arrow. The inch-long quartz projectile point that had killed him was still embedded in the skull upon excavation – exactly where it had struck several centuries earlier. The skull specimen was radiocarbon dated to approximately 1500 A.D. This unfortunate child, it seems, had died a rather brutal death when his village was attacked nearly five hundred years ago.

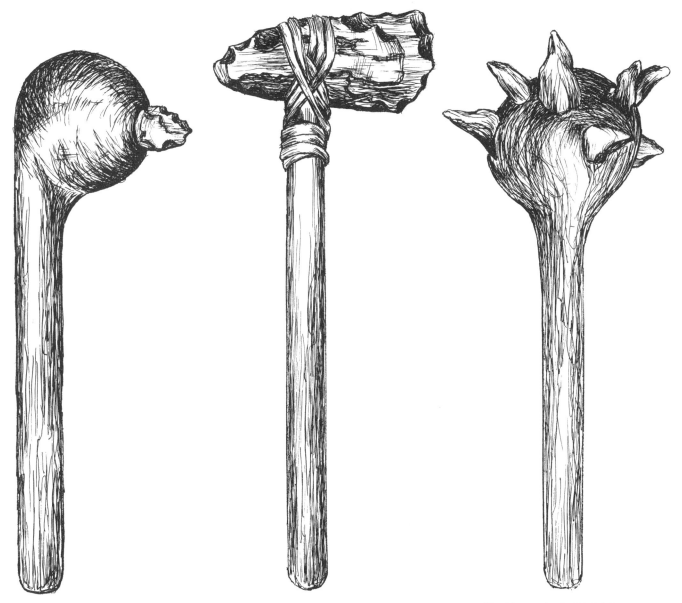

War clubs were tipped with lethal stone prongs, razor-sharp stone hatchet blades, or sharp points carved from tree burls.

RELIGIOUS BELIEFS AND LEGENDS

Among New England's various tribes, religious practices varied according to local custom. Still, they shared many features in common, most notably a profound awe and appreciation for the natural world and its provisions. New England Algonquins were a deeply spiritual people, with a keenly developed sense of reverence. They believed that all of nature, despite its many varied and disparate characteristics, represented a unified whole – the creation of a Supreme Spirit. Every part of His creation – men, beasts, plants, flowers, even pebbles – thus had sacred significance.

To bring indiscriminate harm to an animal or even to a plant was sacrilege to the Indian. He would kill to defend himself, to protect his territory, or to provide food for his family – yet, his religious beliefs forbade him to injure unnecessarily. He would only hunt as many animals or cut down as many trees as he absolutely needed – never more – and he would express thanks in his rituals for that which he had taken. Often, he directly apologized to an animal killed in the hunt, and he wasted none of the creature's flesh or fur, lest its soul return to haunt him for his disrespect and thoughtlessness.

No culture is spiritually flawless. The Indians of New England, like all people in all times, had their share of conflict and war, some of it quite brutal. Yet, such wars were usually caused by territorial infringement; frivolous wars of religious intolerance or ideological difference, so common elsewhere in the world, do not seem to have been characteristic of prehistoric New England culture. With a few exceptions, most tribes were probably not, by nature, warlike. Algonquin spirituality fostered a healthy and genuine respect for all living things.

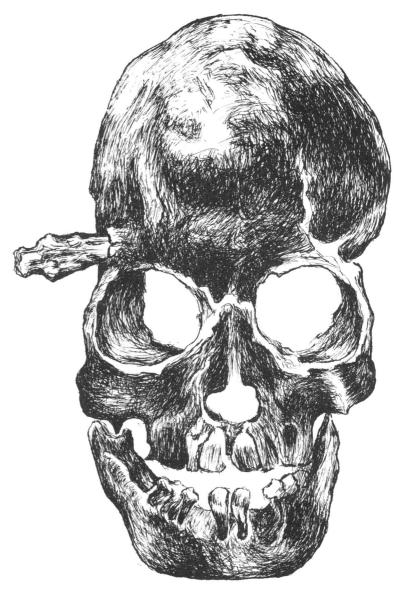

Skull of a young Indian boy, dating to about 1500 A.D., unearthed in 1947 at the Titicut village site by the Taunton River in Massachusetts. Upon excavation, the stone projectile point that had killed this child– perhaps during an attack on his village – was still embedded above his right eye.

Ceramic-Woodland tribes, because of their increasingly stable agricultural food supply, had sufficient leisure time to practice complex, textured religious rituals. Walking along, say, the Taunton River in southeastern Massachusetts on a moonlit summer's eve five or six hundred years ago, one probably would have heard rhythmic drumbeats and beautifully haunting songs and chants. One may have seen Wampanoags, some dressed as colorful feathered birds, others painted with linear patterns and fantastic animal designs, dancing almost convulsively around blazing bonfires, throwing their arms up to the sky, singing to the spirits of their deepest hopes and fears.

While New England's various tribal peoples considered all of nature to be the creation of a single Supreme Spirit (Cautantowwit), their relgious belief system also included a variety of subordinate spiritual entities, or "manitos," which were thought to take a more active role in human affairs than Cautantowwit Himself. Manitos included gods of animals, plants, deceased persons, the sun, moon, earth, sea, sky, fire, water, snow, seasons, winds, directions, and colors. To the Algonquin, the forest was a magical place of many spirits, where trees might whisper eternal secrets, where rocks might cry, and where birds might suddenly transform into luminous rainbows.

The various plant and animal manitos were thought to bring people guidance, hope, comfort, and assistance. Each Indian chose a specific manito to be his or her lifelong guardian. To ask personal favor or forgiveness of one of these manitos, local Indians often relied on their religious specialists (shamans) to serve as human channelers through which the spirit world could be contacted. Algonquins believed that the shaman possessed special spiritual powers, having been called to his profession by a god who appeared to him in a vision, perhaps in the form of a serpent or some other fantastical beast. Any Indian aspiring to such a vision and a career of shamanism usually subjected himself to some lengthy and difficult ordeal, which might include long periods of fasting, loss of sleep,

and drinking herbal mixtures that may have been psychoactive. In such a state, the subject became susceptible to powerful hallucinations, which were interpreted as divine visitation. Subsequently, he became a healer of sorts, whose rituals could bring fellow tribesmen into closer contact with the manitos they wished to address in times of sickness or need.

Ceramic-Woodland tribal beliefs incorporated a number of wonderful myths which aimed to explain some of life's deepest mysteries. Most New England tribes shared similar creation myths:

> When the earth was young, evil spirits unleashed a devastating flood. Some animals escaped a watery death by fleeing to the great mountain in the southwest. There dwelled the great and good god Cautantowwit, also known to various Algonquin tribes as Kiehtan or Woonand. Protected in this mountain-top house, those birds and beasts of the forests had many God-like qualities because of their close association with Him.

> After remaking the mud-soaked earth, Cautantowwit set about to fashion a man and a woman from stone. Dissatisfied with the results, He smashed them into fragments. Again He created a man and a woman, this time from a living tree. He was pleased. Through His handiwork, these humans and their kin possessed immortal souls. He then gave His people general guidelines for living, and corn and beans from His garden. If the Algonquin made the most of his God-given gifts – wisdom, valor, strength, and the like – his soul after death would journey to the great southwest house of Cautantowwit. There he would live in peace and plenty. On the other hand, murderers, thieves, and liars were doomed to restless wandering through eternity.

Wilbur: 69

These petroglyphs – or carved rocks – probably depict various spirit guides – or manitos – and may have been carried for luck. These specimens were recovered from various sites throughout New England.

Algonquin legends, like those of all cultures, reflected deep social and moral concerns. The following tale, variations of which circulated among several New England tribes, is a striking example (for additional Algonquin legends, see Appendix A):

THE INVISIBLE ONE

There was a large Indian village situated on the border of a lake. At the end of the place was a lodge, in which dwelt a being who was always invisible. He had a sister who attended to his wants, and it was known that any girl who could see him might marry him. Therefore there were indeed few who did not make the trial, but it was long before ere one succeeded.

And it passed in this way. Towards evening, when the Invisible One was supposed to be returning home, his sister would walk with any girls who came down to the shore of the lake. She indeed could see her brother, since to her he was always visible, and beholding him she would say to her companions, "Do you see my brother?" and then they would mostly answer, "Yes,...." And then the sister would say, "Of what is his shoulder strap made?".... And they would reply, "A strip of rawhide," or "A green withe," or something of the kind. And then she, knowing they had not told the truth, would reply quietly, "Very well, let us return to the wigwam."

And when they entered the place she would bid them not to take a certain seat, for it was his. And after they had helped to cook the supper they would wait with great curiosity to see him eat. Truly he gave no proof that he was a real person, for as he took off his moccasins they became visible, and his sister hung them up; but beyond this they beheld nothing, not even when they remained all night, as many did.

There dwelt in the village an old man, a widower with three daughters. The youngest of these was very small, weak, and often ill, which did not prevent her sisters, especially the eldest, from treating her with great cruelty. The second daughter was kinder, and sometimes took the part of the poor abused little girl, but the older would burn her hands and face with hot coals; yes, her whole body was scarred with the marks made by torture, so that people called her Oochigeaskw (the burnt-faced girl). And when her father, coming home, asked what it meant that the child was so disfigured, her sister would promptly say that it was the fault of the girl herself, for that, having been forbidden to go near the fire, she had disobeyed and fallen in.

Now it came to pass that it entered into the heads of the two elder sisters of this poor girl that they would go and try their fortune at seeing the Invisible One. So they clad themselves in their finest and strove to look their fairest; and finding his sister at home went with her to take the wonted walk down to the water. Then when he came, being asked if they saw him, they said, "Certainly," and also replied to the question of the shoulder strap, "A piece of rawhide." In saying which, they lied, like the rest, for they had seen nothing, and got nothing for their pains.

When their father returned home the next evening he brought with him many of the pretty little shells form which wampum was made, and they were soon engaged in napawejik (in stringing them).

That day poor little Oochigeaskw, the burnt-faced girl, who had always run barefoot, got a pair of her father's old moccasins, and put them into the water that they might become flexible to wear. And begging her sisters for a few wampum shells, the eldest did call her a "lying little pest," but the other gave her a few. And having no clothes beyond a few paltry rags, the poor creature went forth and got herself from the woods a few sheets of birch bark, of which she made a dress, scraping some figures on the bark. And this dress she shaped like those worn of old. So she made a petticoat and a loose gown, a cap, leggings, and handkerchief, and, having put on her father's great old moccasins – which came up nearly to her knees – she went forth to try her luck. For even this little thing wanted to see the Invisible One in the great wigwam at the end of the village.

Truly her luck had a most inauspicious beginning; there was one long storm of ridicule and hisses, yells and hoots, from her own door to that which she went to seek. Her sisters tried to shame her, and bade her to stay at home, but she would not obey; and all the idlers, seeing this strange little creature in her odd array, cried, "Shame!" But she went on, for she was greatly resolved; it may be that some spirit had inspired her.

Now this poor small wretch in her mad attire, with her hair singed off and her little face as full of burns and scars as there are holes in a sieve, was, for all this, most kindly received by the sister of the Invisible One; for this noble girl knew more than the mere outside of things as the world knows them. And as the brown of the evening sky became black, she took her down to the lake. And erelong the girls knew that he had come. Then the sister said, "Do you see him?" And the other girl replied with awe, "Truly I do – and He is wonderful." "And what is his shoulder strap?" "It is," she replied, "the Rainbow."

"Thou hast seen him," said the sister. And, taking the girl home, she bathed her, and as she washed her all the scars disappeared from face and body. Her hair grew again; it was very long, and like a blackbird's wing. Her eyes were like stars. In all the world there was no such beauty. Then from her treasures she gave her a wedding garment, and adorned her. Under the comb, as she combed her, her hair grew. It was a great marvel to behold.

Then, having done this, she bade her take the wife's seat in the wigwam – that by which her brother sat, the seat next to the door. And when he entered, terrible and beautiful...she became his wife.

As quoted in Leland: 303

MEDICINE AND HEALING

New England's various Ceramic-Woodland tribes possessed vast and comprehensive pharmacological knowledge. They effectively utilized a variety of herbs, plants, and extracts to treat numerous ills, and some of these medicinals are still in use today (which hazel, aspirin, and cannabis, for instance). In times of sickness, Indians could turn to nature the way we might turn to a pharmacy. From plant sources, they skillfully prepared cough and cold remedies, antiseptics, astringents, emetics, carthartics, diaphoretics, stimulants, narcotics, alternatives, and vermifuges. Developed entirely in a wilderness setting, Indian medicine is deserving of respect. It was apparently more advanced than that of the white colonists who would soon reach New England.

In general, local Indians were of robust and exceptional physical health, no doubt due to their clean, spacious, non-urban environment. Old World infectious diseases such as smallpox, typhus, malaria, tuberculosis, measles, diphtheria, and probably syphilis were unknown in prehistoric New England. Because of the versatile Algonquin diet, deformities due to malnutrition, such as rickets and hunchback, were also absent. Obesity was rare, infant mortality low, and life-span generally long (based on excavated burials and the study of associated skeletal remains, an average life-span of sixty seems a good estimate, though there were certainly cases in which individuals lived into their seventies, eighties, and even past a hundred).

Indians took a number of preventative measures against potential health problems. They washed frequently in lakes and streams and anointed their bodies with fish oil or coon grease for protection against sun and insects. They used walnut oil to dress their hair and give it a sheen. The healthful effects of sweat baths, which we have discussed earlier, were especially enjoyed.

In cases of serious injury, the sufferer's family usually called upon the shaman to elicit the assistance of a healing deity, since sickness was thought to be a manifestation of malevolent or angry spirits. Indians considered morality and physical health to be highly interactive, believing that offenses against animals, plants, or other persons could bring ill health to the perpetrator. Considering that human guilt is such a powerful emotion – one that can potentially have physiological implications (loss of appetite, sleep, etc.) – its prospective association with physical illness was not always without validity. In those instances, it was up to the shaman to convince the patient of divine forgiveness – a role not unlike that of the modern-day priest.

The shaman, often donning a colorful animal costume that was representative of a particular healing deity or manito, performed a variety of bizarre rituals around his patient, perhaps even a full exorcism in cases where possession was suspect as the cause of illness. These rituals often included chanting and drum-pounding which – far from simply being used for dramatic effect – were undoubtedly quite effective in diverting the patient's mind from his pain. Spiritual reassurance also allowed the patient to further relax, thereby affording his body more strength for actual physical recovery. Thus, the shaman's healing rituals incorporated crucial psychological components. In some cases, he served as a psychiatrist of sorts, who listened to problems and offered spiritual advice and comforting rites that could, as noted, convince the patient of divine favor or forgiveness, thereby reducing any worry and guilt that might be underlying the physical condition. Usually, shamans charged a fee for their services, in the form of "tributes" of various items and goods. Like the modern-day physician, their social importance was usually rewarded with tremendous social prestige.

Despite their supernatural aura, the shaman's rituals also incorporated sound medical procedures, including the use of herbal medicines and the sucking out of poisons and pus from snakebites and wounds. Still, the true "doctors" of the tribe were its women, for it was they who were the most knowledgeable in the use of plant curatives for lesser ailments not requiring dramatic shaman magic. When their husbands or children were in pain, they prepared medicinals from wintergreen leaves, which contain aspirin. They employed witch hazel, a liquid extract derived from a shrub, to soothe inflammation – a treatment still used by people today. They skillfully set broken bones with bark and resin cements. For coughs and colds, they prepared soothing chest balms from the inner bark of the black cherry tree. Sarsaparilla was used to assist kidney function. All in all, the Indian pharmacopoeia contained several hundred plant remedies, though they varied from tribe to tribe. (See Appendix D.)

PHYSICAL APPEARANCE

When the English colonists reached New England, they made detailed written observations of Indian appearance and dress, and what they saw probably reflected, to a significant extent, the customary clothing and adornment that Ceramic-Woodland tribal peoples had been wearing for several centuries previously. Thus, while our discussion has not yet reached the period of English colonial contact, we will rely on colonial accounts to delineate the probable appearance of New England's Indians during the pre-colonial tribal period.

Contrary to stereotypical notions of Indians as "red men," Indian skin tone was actually a light tawny or bronzed color. Eventual accounts of "red-skinned" Indians were probably due to the fact that many native people often decorated and painted their bodies, especially their faces, with red, iron-based pigments (additionally, those of

Archaeologists are confused by these curious artifacts, known as "gorgets." Perhaps they were used by shamans during their strange healing rituals.

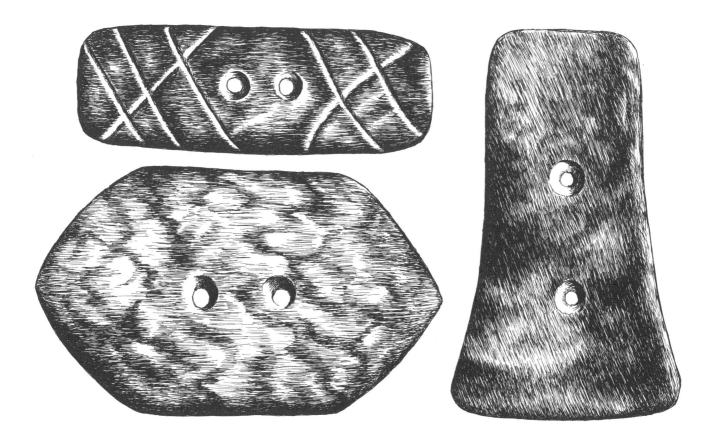

royal or noble blood often tattooed their bodies – usually their cheeks – with certain animal designs, including bears, wolves, and turtles, to designate membership in a particular noble clan or gens – an elite, extended family group, often having its own private section in a village and having a particular animal, or totem, as its symbol. Some nobles chose to burn their clan symbol onto the skin with a hot brand).

Without question, New England Algonquins were a strikingly attractive people. They were tall, lean, muscular, and well-proportioned. High cheekbones, piercing black eyes, smooth, clear skin, and glossy black hair were the rule.

Among men, hair styles varied greatly, although in some tribes boys were not allowed to wear their hair long until the warrior age of sixteen. One popular adult male style (common for Wampanoags, among others) was the "cockscomb" or "mohawk," a single strip of hair running down the center of the head, which was kept short and stiff and was sometimes dyed red. Alternately, a male might wear his hair long, roughly to the shoulders, in which case it was sometimes set into two braids, or decorated with tied-in bits of glistening shell or fanciful stone. In some cases, one side of the head was shaven completely, and the other side left long. Hair was often dressed daily with oil or fat to give it a sheen, and sometimes soot was added to deepen the natural black color.

Indian men seemed to have fussed over their various hair styles more than women, who generally wore their hair long and in braids down the full length of the back, sometimes decorating it with gleaming porcupine quills. Both males and females frequently wore embroidered headbands made from the skin of hawks or other birds. Evidence suggests that warriors sometimes placed eagle or hawk feathers in their headbands, one for each enemy life they had taken in battle, though stereotypical full-feathered head-dresses were western and were not characteristic of New England tribes.

Indian clothing varied with the seasons. In warm weather, dress was light, especially for young children, who often went naked. Both men and women wore breech clouts of doe or seal skin. Men sometimes wore nothing but the breech clout in hot weather; this was often the case with women, also, as they were not ashamed to go topless. Later in the period, women sometimes wore knee-length deerskin skirts and an upper mantle. Men, too, sometimes wore mantle-like shoulder capes to discourage mosquitoes; these were made of woven hemp, or deer or moose skin. When traveling on foot, men and women sometimes protected themselves with leather leggings, which prevented the legs from being scraped by brush and briars along the trail. Both men and women wore buckskin or moosehide moccasins, and females were especially fond of enhancing theirs with dyed designs. In winter, clothing became heavier, and often consisted of furs – beaver, otter, squirrel, and lynx, among others – or hide clothing with fur lining.

TRANSPORTATION

Wooden canoes, as noted earlier, provided a valuable means of water transportation. Rivers allowed access to hard-to-reach hunting grounds and campsites. Occasionally, during warfare between rival tribes, there were "naval battles" in which warriors engaged each other in dugout or birch-bark canoes.

Rivers, however, were not the only native New England "highways." Ceramic-Woodland tribes, throughout their respective territories, created vast networks of land trails that connected villages, hunting grounds, lakes, ponds, and valleys. These well-trodden paths crisscrossed all of New England. They were used for sending messages, hunting, and recreational excursions – and for interaction between villages.

Some male hairstyles worn in various New England tribes.

Tribes laid their trails on the best and most practical inter-territorial routes. For this reason, many of our roads today have been constructed directly over these earlier Indian paths. For instance, Route 44 in southeastern Massachusetts – running from Middleboro, through Taunton and Rehoboth, and into Providence, sits atop a long foot trail used centuries ago by the Wampanoags.

RECREATION AND GAMES

Due to their stable agricultural food supply, Ceramic-Woodland Indians had sufficient leisure time to incorporate numerous sports and games into tribal life. As noted earlier, males engaged in a number of sporting tournaments that kept them physically fit for battle. Frequently, younger females also participated in some of these games. Public sporting exhibitions were usually held in summer, when large numbers of Indians from different villages gathered for a few weeks of fishing and socializing at a favorite waterfall or coastal spot. Here, they held athletic contests that included swimming, running, wrestling, weight-lifting, and marksmanship.

A favored sporting tournament was a type of ball game (modern-day lacrosse is its derivative) which was played between two teams,

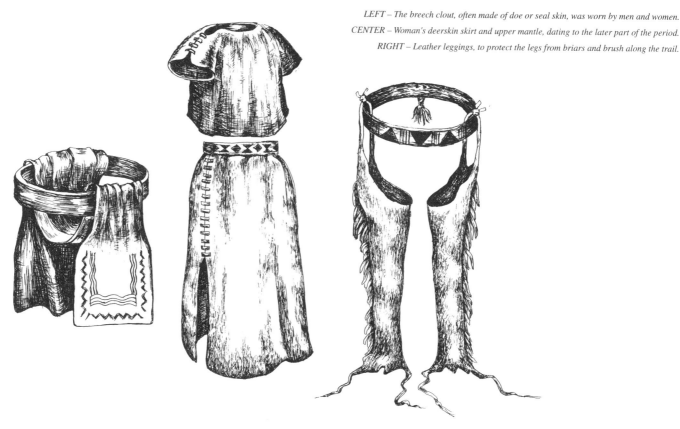

LEFT – The breech clout, often made of doe or seal skin, was worn by men and women.
CENTER – Woman's deerskin skirt and upper mantle, dating to the later part of the period.
RIGHT – Leather leggings, to protect the legs from briars and brush along the trail.

usually on a large stretch of beach, with as much as a mile between the goal posts of each team. Players (sometimes running into the hundreds) used wooden-framed scoops meshed with leather lacing to toss about a small deerskin ball stuffed with animal hair. Players on each team passed to each other and tried to carry the ball to the opposing team's goal, where it was flung past the posts to score a point. Interaction between opposing players also involved body checking and wrestling each other to the ground. Single games sometimes lasted several days, with prizes of valuable furs or wampum-shell necklaces going to the eventual winners. Spectators often engaged in a significant amount of wagering; at the game's end, some of them left practically naked, hav-

ing bet away all of their belongings, including their clothes.

Other popular tournaments included tug-of-wars and contests with gaming stones (rounded, disk-like stones that were rolled into a large playing area; the object was for each player to hurl an eight-foot pole as close as possible to the spot where he or she believed the rolling stone would come to rest. The pole landing closest to the actual spot won its thrower a prize of furs and wampum, paid by the losers). In addition to public contests, there were also lesser games that both men and women could enjoy in the privacy of their wig-wams. Dice games, for instance, were quite popular.

CONCLUSIONS

At this point in our discussion, it should be apparent that Ceramic-Woodland tribal life eventually became, as the period progressed, an increasingly structured, well-organized existence of an intelligent and creative people who enjoyed life and lived it well. The advent of agriculture and its attendant stabilization of the food supply led to increased population, the gradual establishment of stable agricultural villages in many parts of New England, and the eventual emergence of distinct tribal groupings as villages within various territories formally banded together to protect their part of the region from intrusion. An increasingly settled (although not completely sedentary) existence meant the gradual advancement of certain non-material cultural traits – most notably, increasingly structured political, social, and religious systems.

However, these new advances still had a long way to go, and they would ultimately not have the chance. Although a fully settled agricultural and village society was well in the making, it would be rudely interrupted and thwarted by a 17th-century influx of English settlers into New England. Almost overnight, a culture that had begun to brilliantly flourish would instead be on its way to complete dissolution.

Chapter Five

The Historic-Contact Period
1600-1676

FIRST EUROPEANS

Prior to the establishment of the English colony at Plymouth in 1620, a few European explorers and traders had, for almost a century previously, been making brief cruises along the New England coastline (a few researchers suggest that exploring vessels from Europe and the Mediterranean had been making visits to New England since as early as 1500 B.C. While this controversial and academically unpopular view is intriguing, it has yet to be substantiated beyond a reasonable doubt). The first documented visit was that of the Italian navigator Giovanni Verrazzano in 1524. Verrazzano, in the service of Francis I of France, was searching for an all-water route through North America to China.

After sailing up past the Carolinas and New York, he dropped anchor at Point Judith. Almost immediately, a group of Indians (probably Wampanoags) paddled out to his ship, and Verrazzano was struck by their eager curiosity and friendliness. With their guidance, the Italian adventurer navigated his ship into Rhode Island's Narragansett Bay, where he again dropped anchor in what is now Newport Harbor. He and his crew remained for two weeks, venturing ashore to survey the mainland, which Verrazzano called "as pleasant as possible to conceive." He noted lush woods of oak and walnut and such game as lynx and deer, as well as fertile open plains cleared by the Indians, some "as much as twenty or thirty leagues in length, entirely free from trees."

Verrazzano's writings offer us a most revealing glimpse into the character and disposition of the local Indians. A curious ship of immense size appears off their coast. It is like nothing they have seen previously. On its deck there are unusual, pale-skinned men dressed in bizarre attire. Yet, the Indians do not fear this peculiar sight or retreat from it. Rather, they directly and boldly approach. They are not aroused to anxious hostility; they are not stirred to violence by that which is unfamiliar or different. They do not attempt to use their vastly superior numbers to capture the huge and wondrous "canoe" now anchored off their coast. Rather, their first and only response is to offer help.

Throughout the remainder of the sixteenth and early seventeenth centuries, New England was visited by additional French, Dutch, and English explorers and traders. By 1607, small numbers of them had established a few temporary commercial fishing posts in northern New England, and additional Europeans continued to make brief explorations of more southerly locales along the New England coastline before the arrival of the Pilgrims. While there were occasional skirmishes with the natives – sometimes the result of Indians being cheated in trading – the vast majority of New England Algonquins were, at this point, little affected by this minor foreign presence. For the moment, they faced a much more apparent threat from the powerful Iroquois Indian Confederacy of New York, which was taking an increasingly threatening posture toward New England and whose various tribes had already begun to invade parts of Vermont and Connecticut. In time, however, even the dangers posed by the aggressive Iroquois would be far outweighed by those of the white man. In fact, within the next seventy years, English settlers would virtually exterminate the entirety of New England Native American culture.

In Massachusetts, before the colonists had even established a single settlement in this part of New England, their diseases were already killing off a good part of the Indian populace. Beginning about 1616, the local Wampanoags were struck by a devastating plague. The quickness with which the disease hit and spread suggests that it was a virus to which the Indians had never been previously exposed and against which they had no immunity. In all likelihood, the sickness was smallpox (or, as some researchers have recently suggested, bubonic plague), and it took a horrendous toll on the local population, though the Rhode Island Narragansetts somehow managed to escape contraction (giving them a dangerous military advantage over the Wampanoags, with whom they were again in conflict at this time). Exactly how the disease was introduced is uncertain, though it probably derived from a small European exploring party that had briefly come ashore in southern New England, or from the several surviving crew members of a French ship that was wrecked on Cape Cod about 1616.

PLYMOUTH COLONY AND SUBSEQUENT PURITAN SETTLEMENT

In the fall of 1620, while the local Wampanoags were still reeling from their losses, a small group of English Pilgrims (Puritan separatists from the Church of England) established the first permanently settled Anglo-American colony at Plymouth, Massachusetts. When they first landed, the Pilgrims found evidence of former Indian occupation at Plymouth, though the population of this particular village site (known as Patuxet) was now gone, having completely succumbed to the plague. However, one Indian from the former Plymouth village had managed to escape the earlier onslaught of disease. His name was Squanto and he, along with another Indian named Samoset, who had learned English from European fishermen in Maine, approached the new Pilgrim settlement the following spring, after a ravaging winter had decimated the small English population, killing off about half.

Squanto and his companion did nothing less than teach the new colonists how to keep from starving to death in their new environment. Had it not been for this Indian assistance, the Pilgrims quite possibly would have been forced to sail home. Under the guidance of Squanto and Samoset, the English learned how to work the unfamiliar New England soil and fertilize their crops with fish. "In this feature of agriculture as well as others, the New England Algonquins were the experts and the English became their pupils (Russell, 166)."

After their friendly initial dealings with Squanto and Samoset, the Pilgrims soon dispatched a delegation (perhaps using the ancient footpath now covered by Route 44) to establish contact with Massasoit, the Wampanoag sachem, who was residing with his people at Mount Hope. Massasoit immediately extended a welcoming hand to the English newcomers, with whom he signed a peace treaty that would last some fifty years. An inter-cultural relationship of mutual cooperation ensued between the Wampanoags and the Pilgrims, who gathered together at Plymouth for a great Thanksgiving feast after the fall harvest of 1621. However:

> This remarkable cooperative alliance of two very disparate cultures was, from the start, illusory. Though a superficial inter-racial peace did persist for a good number of years...and though a few colonists wrote quite favorably of the local natives...many more remained apprehensive and loathsome of an alternate culture they could neither comprehend nor predict. The friendly goings-on at Plymouth were likely rooted in utility, and, for the most part, they do not seem to reflect a substantive Pilgrim respect for the Indian people.... With a few notable exceptions, the English settlers deemed the Indian populace to be a culturally, morally, and intellectually inferior one. William Bradford, one of Plymouth

Colony's founders, perhaps best expressed true underlying Pilgrim sentiment when he wrote that Indians are '...savage and brutish...little otherwise than wild beasts....' In his arrogance, Bradford apparently overlooked the fact that these same 'wild beasts' had graciously taught the Plymouth colonists how to keep from starving to death in their new environment.

Robinson: (3); 11

Under the governorship of Bradford, Plymouth Colony slowly grew, sustained in part by periodic influxes of new white settlers sailing from England. While the initial settlement of Plymouth was supposed to see all land held and worked in common for the first seven years, residents increasingly clamored for their own private parcels, and Bradford eventually assigned every man, woman, and child one acre for their own use, with the remainder of land still held in common.

By the 1630's, however, the land situation was becoming increasingly precarious, since waves of Puritan settlers were now arriving from England by the thousands. While these new Puritan arrivals established their own colony to the north of Massachusetts Bay (Massachusetts Bay Colony), its geographical boundaries were less well-defined than those of Plymouth Colony, and Puritan families quickly spread themselves throughout Massachusetts. As more and more English poured into the colony, land became an increasingly precious commodity. Unlike the Indians who had held land communally for thousands of years, the English sought private ownership of theirs, and this meant taking it out of the hands of the local Indians.

The Puritans established one Massachusetts town after another, and they frequently did so at the great expense of the local Indian populace. Tensions gradually escalated:

When obtaining land from the Indians, the whites often managed to defraud them, leading to animosity. Even when transactions were honorable, problems resulted from the Indians' failure to grasp the subtleties of English law and the concept of individual ownership, an idea alien to them. As far as the Indians were concerned, when they put their marks on deeds, they were granting permission to the colonists for use of the land, not ceding their own hunting and fishing rights.

But there were other issues as well, other areas of conflict. The expanding European presence also meant the disolution of Indian culture and the erosion of the Indians' economic base. Colonial missionaries zealously sought to convert the 'pagans' to Christianity, creating a large number of 'Praying Indians,' and along with them a stressful cultural rift within Indian society. Meanwhile, English traders effected the economic subjugation of the Indians, making them dependent on European goods and at the same time saddling them with debt.... The resulting proximity of Indian to white led to frequent quarrels over money, possessions, and insults imagined or real – some of which escalated into acts of violence.

When Indians committed some infraction under English law, they were dragged before colonial courts, a procedure which itself seemed an injustice to them. They were accountable to their own people, the Indians believed, not to the Crown, and certainly not to the Puritan 'blue laws.' For the New England Indian, humiliation piled upon humiliation, resentment upon resentment.

Waldman: 91

The establishment of Rehoboth, Massachusetts, in 1643 serves as a good example of questionable fairness on the part of the colonists when negotiating land deals with the local Indians. Sections of Rehoboth had, for centuries, served as hunting grounds for the local Wampanoags, and its lands represented a significant part of their claimed territorial domain. Yet, the colonial settlers of Rehoboth managed to wrest all of its lands (which, at that time, included not only present-day Rehoboth, but also Seekonk, East Providence, and Pawtucket) from the Wampanoags for a most paultry sum. "...Old Rehoboth was bought of Massassoit for ten fathoms of wampum, equal at that time to fifty shillings, with a coat thrown in (Tilton: 65)."

Massasoit, like many other tribal chiefs, was willing to accept such meager compensation for large tracts of land because he did not yet understand that he was relinquishing his own rights to those lands, not just selling the colonists a share in their use. Not bothering to explain English property laws to the Indians with whom they were transacting, many colonists were relying on misunderstanding and misinformation to pull off questionable land deals:

During the 1600's, therefore, the Puritans were the beneficiaries of some outstanding real-estate bargains, for it has been estimated that the entire state of Massachusetts could have been purchased for less than $2,500.00 based on those early rates paid to the Indians. Furthermore, some of the settlers were not satisfied with the bargains they received and sometimes yielded to the temptation of claiming much more land than had been agreed upon in

An iron trade ax, one of the many types of European trade goods upon which New England's Indians became increasingly dependent during the 1600's.

the bill-of-sale. The English courts very seldom granted hearings to those Indians who complained of these abuses, for the original boundaries were usually so vaguely defined that it would be practically impossible to arrive at a fair judgment....

(Relations were further marred by the fact that) the English refused to tether their livestock, and the animals frequently foraged in areas that were under cultivation by the...natives. Several who had their crops trampled or eaten by English-owned cattle went to court seeking reparations for the damage, but the body ruled that the plaintiffs were at fault, since they had neglected to fence in their lands. Since the Indians kept their own livestock under constant surveillance, they saw no reason why the English could not do the same...

Bonfanti: 36-39

KING PHILIP

Facing continued Puritan religious repression, disease, land swindles, and cultural assault (which included the introduction of alcohol to the Indians, who had no tolerance to this unfamiliar and disorienting Old World drug and who were sometimes offered it by the colonists during the course of questionable land transactions), many local Indians eventually began to reconsider the peace treaty that Massasoit had signed years earlier with the Plymouth Pilgrims. In effect, that treaty had already been broken, for the thousands of Puritans who had followed the first Pilgrims were already waging nothing less than an undeclared though full-scale cultural war against the increasingly weakened and land-bereft Indians. When Chief Massasoit died in 1662, his son Metacom, also known as Philip, would survey the worsening situation with less peaceable resignation than had his father.

Upon Massasoit's death, the Wampanoag sachemdom passed to his son Alexander (Wampsutta), Philip's elder brother. That same year, however, Alexander suddenly died under suspicious circumstances, and Philip, who had now become the new Wampanoag chief at the age of twenty-two, believed that Alexander had been poisoned by the colonists (he had died, with violent stomach pains, just a short time after being questioned by the English, who apparently suspected him of rebellious ambitions). At the very least, Philip concluded, Alexander had been killed by one of the white man's strange diseases. He grew increasingly bitter over his brother's death, although the most pressing cause of Philip's consternation was mounting Puritan greed. From his tribal seat at Mount Hope, he monitored the progressive and alarming spread of white settlers over the landscape.

The lands of New England were surely plentiful enough for both cultures to coexist with equal shares, and, from the start, the Indians had peaceably welcomed such a prospect. However, it was now obvious to Philip that "shares" were the last thing the colonists had in mind when it came to land. They wanted virtually all of it. Increasingly hemmed in at Mount Hope, Philip and his tribe were now denied access to many parts of the sacred Wampanoag territory that they and their ancestors had been freely wandering for ages. For the first time in one hundred centuries, the Indian populace began to notice the first stone and wooden fences ever erected on New England soil.

Philip was a visionary, a proud and dynamic leader who could see that the future of his people would be no future at all unless it could be wrested from colonial hands. Under his leadership, there was an

The colonists also received certain Indian goods in trade – like this beautifully woven basket – although the commodity that most interested the white settlers was Indian land.

increasingly obvious militancy among the Wampanoags, and the English apparently sensed its presence:

As early as the spring of 1671, the English settlers became alarmed at the evidence they discovered of war-like preparations on the part of King Philip, and they suspected that some plot was on foot for their destruction. There was no documentary proof that such was the case, but numerous strange Indians seen mingling with the Wampanoags, together with Philip's reluctance to meet the colonists at Taunton at their request, excited their suspicions, and they demanded that he appear before them on the 13th of April. Thus coerced, Philip came to Taunton with some of his (assistants). Here he was met by the armed militia of the town, not without hostile demonstrations, but after some parleying it was agreed that a council should be held in the Taunton meeting house, one side of which should be occupied by the English, and the other by the Indians.

The English charged him with plotting rebellion against their government, although the question is pertinent, as one historian has posed it, 'how King Philip, an independent prince and ruler of another nation, could thus rebel.' He was pressed to sign a treaty of allegiance to the King of England and to surrender all guns and ammunition held by the Indians....

At this date bows and arrows had mostly been super-seded by guns, upon which the Indians had come to rely almost exlusively for providing themselves with game for food. To be forced to give up their chief means of livelihood which they had bought from English traders and legally owned...seemed to them nothing less than robbery.

But Philip, swallowing his anger and righteous resentment at such demands, signed the treaty known as "his submission," along with his chief captains, and surrendered what guns the men had with them at the time....

Tilton: 66

In the ensuing months, the English passed even more resolutions aimed at humbling Philip and checking his authority, and Philip submitted to all of them. In reality, however, his compliance was hardly submission. Rather, the Wampanoag sachem was cleverly biding his time, hoping that by signing treaties, surrendering a few guns (though he would by no means surrender all of them), and even giving up more land he could make an overture of peace and thus allay the colonists' suspicions. In this manner, he lulled the English into a false sense of security and proceeded with developing his plans over the next few years. His goal was to patch up old differences with the Narragansetts and other Indians in order to attain a tribal alliance. He was a prudent strategist who knew that any Indian resistance would have to be well-coordinated and, to the greatest extent possible considering that a good many Indians were now "Praying Indians" sympathetic to the English, unified.

Philip's emissaries worked diligently at winning the support of some of the other New England tribes, with varying degrees of success (in time, the Wampanoags would succeed in securing their most important allies, the Narragansetts, who numbered some 4,000. Alone, Philip's tribe numbered about 1,200). Despite the impatience of many Indians to commence hostilities at once, Philip planned a first strike against the English for the spring of 1676. The goal was to oust the colonists from New England completely, and he did not want to take on this formidable task too hastily.

Firearms purchased by Indians from European traders quickly supplanted the bow and arrow as a means of hunting – and fighting.

However, hostilities would break out a year earlier than planned, primarily due to the treachery of John Sassamon (or Sausamon), a native of Dorchester and the son of "Praying Indians." Sassamon, though he had been educated by the English and had worked for them as a missionary among the Namasket Indians of Middleboro, had at some point been an advisor to King Philip at Mount Hope. As such, he had eventually learned of Philip's plans. However, in the winter of 1675, he supposedly betrayed Philip to the English and, several days later, he disappeared. His body was eventually found in Lake Assowompsett in Middleboro, with injuries indicative of murder:

> Three Indians were arrested by the English and executed, two of whom denied all knowledge of the act, but one confessed. One of the three was Tobias, a counselor of King Philip. Probably Philip, on discovering Sassamon's treachery, condemned him to death after the Indian fashion. This execution of his subjects by the English seemed to Philip a meddlesome interference with the course of Indian justice, and so exasperated him that he now threw off all disguise and pushed his preparations as diligently as possible.
>
> Tilton: 67.

THE OUTBREAK OF KING PHILIP'S WAR

Philip still hoped to delay hostilities a bit longer so that his people would be adequately prepared. However, outraged by the English execution of Tobias and the others, his warriors had grown even more impatient. On June 20, 1675, several came into Swansea and began to harass the English by burning houses and killing cattle. On June 23, Swansea resident John Salisbury, a young man of about twenty, shot at several Indians, on the orders of his father, William Salisbury, who had seen the Indians fleeing from his property. John's shots mortally wounded one of them. The following day, the Indians launched a full attack on Swansea, killing or mortally wounding nine white residents and also apprehending John and his father, who were executed and whose bodies were decapitated.

Thus commenced King Philip's War, which would, over the next fourteen months, cost the lives of some six hundred Englishmen – along with the lives of several thousand Indians – and would result in the burnings of over a thousand colonial barns, homes, and mills in various parts of New England. During the ordeal, the townspeople of southeastern New England – especially southeastern Massachusetts and Rhode Island – would be especially vulnerable to hostile Indian raids, because of the fairly close proximity of Philip's headquarters at Mount Hope. Towns like Rehoboth, Swansea, and Taunton were kept in an almost constant state of alarm. Many residents had to abandon their homes and were forced to take up protective residence in one of a number of guarded garrison houses.

FIRST SKIRMISHES OF THE WAR

Just before the initial Swansea hostilities, English officials had been parleying with Philip, and an avoidance of war seemed at least somewhat possible. However, after the Swansea attack of June 24, Philip realized that he could no longer hold back his warriors. In the meantime, the incidents in Swansea had quickly stirred the English to begin military mobilization of forces from both Massachusetts and Plymouth Colonies.

The Massachusetts Colony forces left Boston on June 26 and 27 and included a company of foot soldiers led by Captain David Henchman, a calvalry troop under Captain Thomas Prentice, and a volunteer foot company of about a hundred men commanded by Captain Samuel Mosely (the commander-in-chief of all of these Boston forces was Major Thomas Savage, who would join them a few days later).

On the 26th, the first two companies marched from Boston to the Woodcock Garrison in Attleboro, Massachusetts, where they were joined by Mosely's forces on the 27th. This entire army then marched on to Swansea, Massachusetts, where they met the troops from Plymouth Colony, under the command of Major James Cudworth, who had been waiting for them at Swansea's Miles Garrison. While waiting in Swansea for the Boston troops to arrive, Cudworth's Plymouth forces had already been shot at by the Indians, though the men, women, and children of Rehoboth and Swansea had been safely placed in the local garrison houses by this time:

The inaction of the Plymouth Colony forces while awaiting the Boston reinforcements made the Indians so bold that, in the language of Captain (Benjamin) Church, 'they shot down two sentinels under the very noses of the soldiers occupying Miles Garrison.' They were lying in wait on every side to kill all that went abroad. But on the arrival of the (Boston troops), twelve of (Prentice's) men...ventured a forward movement, and taking with them Wm. Hammond as pilot, they crossed over to the east side of the Palmer's River, when they were fired upon from an ambuscade, and their pilot was mortally wounded. (Another) was also wounded, having his horse shot under him, and a musket-ball ploughed its way through (a corporal's) buff coat. So terrified were the troopers by their first taste of actual warfare that they fled panic-striken back to (the Miles Garrison); and but for the bravery of Benjamin Church, who was in the party and who was wounded in the foot, they would have left their wounded companion and their dead pilot in the hands of the enemy (Captain Church pursuaded some of the men to return with him to retrieve them).

Tilton: 70.

The next morning, June 29, the Massachusetts and Plymouth Colony troops headed for Philip's Mount Hope, Rhode Island, headquarters:

The Indians appeared at the edge of the swamps, trying to lure the men into chasing them. Mosely led his entire company after them, and his show of bravery encouraged several others to follow after him. As this last group entered Mount Hope Neck, they heard Mosely's men floundering about nearby. Thinking they had come upon a band of Indians, they fired at them, and Mosely's men returned the fire. Before they had realized their mistake, several men were killed and a number of others severely wounded.

Bonfanti: 61

After this incident of "friendly fire," the troops marched forward and came upon a grisly sight:

> ...they came to the narrow of (Mount Hope) neck, (and), at a place called Keekamuit, or Kickemuit (present-day Warren, R.I.), they found the heads of eight Englishmen, that the Indians had murdered, set upon poles by the side of the way. These they took down and buried. On arriving at Mount Hope the troops found that Philip and his Indians had left the place (had fled to Pocasset, present-day Tiverton). They erected a fort on Mount Hope Neck, and leaving in it a garrison of 40 men, the troops...returned the next morning to Swansea.

Bliss: 86

Captain Benjamin Church urged his commanders to lead the troops into Pocasset in pursuit of Philip, who had apparently fled there to elicit military assistance from the Pocasset Indians (a minor Rhode Island tribe, significantly smaller than the Narragansetts, but still offering a good number of prospective warriors, whose support Philip succeeded in winning). Instead, thinking that there were still Indians in the immediate area, the English commanders ordered the troops to conduct useless sorties in the swamps about Mount Hope, Swansea, and Rehoboth over the next few days. They found nothing, aside from a small group of Indians who were caught burning a house in Rehoboth. The English fired upon the group, killing four and losing one of their own to return fire.

Map delineating Mount Hope, Rhode Island (King Philip's tribal headquarters) and environs. The first skirmishes of King Philip's War took place in this area. Note Miles Garrison (in Swansea, Massachusetts) at upper left corner of map.

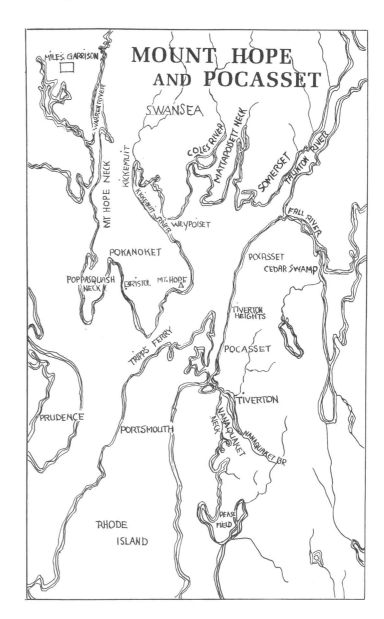

78

THE POCASSET SWAMP AMBUSH

Finally, in mid-July, the combined Plymouth and Massachusetts forces moved into Pocasett, Rhode Island, in pursuit of Philip. Philip and his main band had taken refuge in a deep swamp, which prevented the English from making a direct attack. Captain Henchman ordered his troops to construct a fort at the swamp's edge, hoping the Indians would thus be prevented from moving and would be subdued by starvation.

Philip realized that he would have to flee once again, and by so doing, he hoped to draw the English into an ambush:

> ...(Philip) recognized the gravity of his situation, for a large force could keep him pinned down in a small area until he was either starved into submission or was killed. Accordingly, he made plans to cross the Taunton River to the relative safety of Nipmuck Country. Sunconewhew, his younger brother and his leading war captain, volunteered to protect the rear, allowing the main body of Indians to cross the river, while he (would fight) against any troops that might try to stop them.

> On July 18, while the cross was taking place, Sunconewhew positioned his men on both sides of a narrow path over which the English would have to come if they pursued the fleeing Indians. Although the soldiers had no knowledge of the planned exodus, a large (number of English) happened to be patrolling this particular area that day, and when they blundered into the ambush, they were met with a volley of shots that instantly killed five

To the left: During the first days of the war, eight severed English heads were encountered by colonial forces at Mount Hope Neck (present-day Warren, Rhode Island). It was now apparent to the colonists that the Indians meant serious business.

of them and wounded several more. Due to the heavy foliage, there was very little light, and the demoralized soldiers were unable to tell from which direction the bullets were coming. They confusedly began to fire at each other, succeeding in killing some of their own comrades before the mistake was discovered. The Indians moved about constantly, making it difficult for the soldiers to find targets to shoot at, and when the soldiers at last retreated, they left behind them a large number of dead and wounded (about fifteen English were killed; three Indians died in the skirmish, including Philip's younger brother, Sunconewhew).

Bonfanti: 63

Philip and his large party (which included women and children) successfully escaped across the Taunton River and headed northwest toward the tribal territory of the numerous Nipmuck Indians (who occupied the Worcester area and whose support Philip sought to strengthen). As they crossed the Seekonk Plain, Philip and his band were "discovered by the people of Rehoboth, who, headed by the Reverend Noah Newman, their minister, and accompanied by a small party of Mohegans (a Connecticut tribe sympathetic to the English), gave a close and brisk pursuit, killing twelve of his men... (Bliss: 87)." Still, Philip and most of his band managed to escape, eventually making their way into the land of the numerous Nipmucks. For the time being, Philip and his band were out of immediate danger.

PHILIP THE COWARD?

At this point, the reader has probably noticed that Philip always seems to be in retreat. In fact, Philip's strategy for himself and his own band was primarily elusive. Throughout most of the war, the fighting, raiding, and burning were done by satellite Wampanoag warrior bands that were separated from Philip's band, along with ally war parties of Narragansetts, Nipmucks, and other Indians. However, the charge of cowardice that has been leveled at Philip by some commentators "is based on a misconception of his tactics. No one knew better than (Benjamin) Church...that his arch enemy was 'always foremost in flight.' But (in his diary on the war) it never occurred to him to hold that to Philip's discredit (LCHS: 29-30)."

Philip's movements reflect a recognition on his part that the most important role he could play in his own cause was that of diplomat. While there were many young men who could serve as warriors, he, as tribal sachem, could best negotiate with other tribes for their assistance. Hence, his first movement took him to Pocasset, were he won the support of many warriors among that tribe, and then he moved into Nipmuck territory to strengthen the pro-war faction among those people. If Philip was constantly retreating from the English, it was perhaps because he believed that he was of most value to his people alive, as a powerful agent of inter-tribal negotiation. As a dead warrior, he might be a hero to his people, but he would be of little practical use to them. Additionally, Indian fighting tactics in general rarely emphasized head-on confrontation in the open, but rather relied on quick, surprise strikes followed by fast retreats.

THE GREAT SWAMP FIGHT

After Philip safely disappeared into Nipmuck country, the English turned their attention to the numerous Rhode Island Narragansetts, whose support of Philip's revolt would soon cost them dearly:

> In December, 1675, the Narragansett Indians had gone into winter quarters at South Kingston, R.I. Their rendezvous was an immense fort on an island of five or six acres in the center of a swamp. This fortress was surrounded by high palisades, with the entrance at one quarter having a sort of blockhouse and flankers. The space within the fort area was dotted with wigwams, in which were gathered all the old men, women, and children of the Narragansett tribe, besides many refugees of the Wampanaoags and Pocassets. It is stated that more than 3,000 Indians were spending the winter in this fortified retreat.
>
> Tilton: 73

About fifteen hundred English troops under the command of Major Josias Winslow, along with two hundred Mohegan Indian sympathizers, attacked the Narragansett fort on December 19th, during a snow storm. The Indians fired a barrage of musket shots, killing several officers and numerous troops at the head of the charge. The English pressed forward, however, and were soon able to penetrate the stronghold. For about three hours, the bloody encounter raged on, until the snow on the ground was stained bright red and heaps of bodies lay strewn about the fort. Finally, as the Indian warriors began to retreat, the English set fire to all of the wigwams, tragically burning alive many of the non-combatants, including women, children, and elderly Indians. The slaughter was the worst atrocity of the war. Total Indian losses were staggering – probably about six hundred killed, with another three hundred taken captive. Losses on the English side totalled about three hundred, with many more wounded.

The English had dealt the Narragansetts a cruel and terrible blow (though they had not managed to capture their chief sachem, Canonchet, a keen strategist who would direct many of the subsequent Indian attacks against the English). So horrendous was this English atrocity that present-day Narragansetts "...still tell successive generations of the outrageous nature of the assault. Like Pearl

Harbor, it will never be forgotten. 'So far as we're concerned' (said one modern-day Narragansett leader), 'what the Puritans began here has never ended. The war is still on' (Bourne: 153)."

PIERCE'S FIGHT

Far from eliminating the Narragansett threat, the English attack on the South Kingston village had only served to intensify it. By the late winter and early spring 1676, many Narragansetts who had not been caught in the Great Swamp Fight, along with other Indian war parties in the area, dispersed into numerous raiding bands and began to aggressively assault a number of towns in both Massachusetts and Rhode Island in retaliation for the outrageous slaughter committed by the English. Some of the worst of these attacks were orchestrated by the aggressive Narragansett sachem Canonchet, who by now was thirsty for revenge:

> On 25 Dec. 1676, they attacked the deserted town of Weymouth and burned seven or eight houses and barns and killed one or two persons. In the beginning of the month of March 1676, they burned twelve houses at Pawtucket, most of which were in the township of Rehoboth (Old Rehoboth).

> By 12 March 1676, the Indians had penetrated within two miles of the village of Plymouth where at Eel River they burned the house of Capt. William Clark, murdered Mrs. Sarah Clark, an infant, and some eight or nine persons from other families...

> On 13 March 1676, about 400 Indians attacked Groton, Mass., burning about forty dwellings and other buildings and killing some of the inhabitants. On 17 March 1676, the Indians burned all but a few of the hous-

es left standing at Warwick, near Providence, killing one man, and burned the houses of the English remaining in the Narragansett country.

Bowen: III; 12

The increasing ferocity of Indian violence again became apparent when an English expedition of about fifty colonial troops, along with an additional twenty Christian Indians, was viciously ambushed while patrolling for marauding Indians. Captain Michael Pierce of Scituate, Plymouth Colony, had command of the company, which he led to Rehoboth (Old Rehoboth) where, on March 26, about three miles northwest of the present Newman Congregational Church (in modern-day East Providence, Rhode Island), a terrible encounter ensued:

> ...in an obscure, woody place, (Pierce and his men) discovered a few rambling Indians who seemed in haste to get away but limped as if they had been seriously wounded. These men the English pursued and soon found them to be decoys leading them into an ambuscade. Suddenly, Captain Pierce found himself in the presence of an overwhelming force of the enemy.... At one point the 500 Indians surrounding him seemed to give ground, but when 400 more came up, they outnumbered his (70) men (more than ten to one). The English, forming a circle, made a brave resistance for about two hours, during which time Captain Pierce...(and) 52 English soldiers were slain besides 11 friendly Indians.

Tilton: 76

Many historians have suggested that Canonchet personally directed this ambush. Though Pierce and most of his company were killed in the attack, they had managed, during their two hour resistance, to kill over a hundred of the enemy, an amazing feat considering they were only seventy men against almost a thousand. Among those few in Pierce's company who did manage to escape were three "friendly" Indians fighting on the side of the English. Leonard Bliss, Jr., in his *History Of Rehoboth (1836)*, relates several interesting anecdotes concerning the escapes made by these three:

> One being closely pursued by a hostile Indian, sought shelter behind a large rock. Thus the two were watching, in awful suspense, to shoot each other. But Captain Pierce's Indian, putting his hat on the end of his gun, raised it to the view of his enemy, who immediately fired at the (hat), and the next moment was shot dead by the friendly Indian. Another, in his flight, pretended to pursue an Englishman with an uplifted tomahawk, holding it in a threatening attitude above his head, and thus escaped (along with the Englishman). A third, being closely pursued, took shelter behind the roots of a tree that had been lately turned out of the ground; and the hostile Indian, coming up on the other side, was lying in wait to shoot him upon deserting his station; when the friendly Indian, boring a hole through his broad shield, unobserved by the other, shot him dead.

Bliss: 91

INDIAN TERROR

On March 28, two days after the crushing English defeat in Pierce's Fight, some fifteen hundred Indians, under the leadership of Canonchet, burned most of the remaining barns and houses in Rehoboth. "These houses were around the 'Ring of the town.' The garrison houses (were) spared, (along with) another house at the south end of the Common which had black sticks set up around it to look like sentinels. Tradition says that the houses were kindled early in the evening, so that when the sun arose the next morning it beheld a circle of smoking ruins (Tilton: 78)." One Rehoboth resident, Robert Beers, an Irish brick-maker, was killed in the attack; the others had earlier fled the area or had sought refuge in one of the local garrison houses.

The following day, March 29, the Indians crossed the Seekonk River and set fire to Providence, Rhode Island. Again, only one person was killed, a man named Wright. Refusing to flee and trusting his Bible to save him, Wright was soon killed by attacking Indians who "ripped him open and put his Bible in his belly (Bowen: III; 17)."

Roving Indian war bands then proceeded to make attacks on a number of English towns, including Billerica, Andover, Hingham, and Weymouth, resulting in more civilian deaths. It is hard to imagine the terror that gripped New England at this time. It was a "frightful drama of Indian warhoop, sudden attack, flaming dwelling houses, and atrocious massacres (Bowen: III; 1)." What probably most terrified the colonists was the prospect of Indians suddenly appearing out of nowhere, for they were masters at "...the stealthy approach (and) the whirling attack...Imagine the feeling of the householder encircled by the forest: 'They know where we are! We never know where they are!' (LCHS: 30)." Yet, this war was equally terrifying for the Indians involved, for the English (in the Great Swamp Fight) had demonstrated that they would not shrink from slaughtering women and children. In this war, as in all, there were vicious atrocities committed on both sides.

In general, the English were at a disadvantage because of their inexperience in Indian warfare:

> The essence of Indian warfare was the raid – the
> stealthy approach, the whirling attack, the hand-to-hand

To the right: King Philip's War, a bloody and brutal conflict whose worst battles took place in southeastern New England, ultimately led to the deaths of more than six hundred colonists and several thousand Indians.

combat in which every man fought for himself. The art was for small parties to keep on the move, ambushing, killing, burning; rarely facing a fight in the open without the benefit of surprise; and melting into the swamps before superior force. The English had everything to learn about this kind of fighting, handicapped as they were by their European manuals, their notions of static warfare, and their forty years of peace (since arriving).

LCHS: 30

Still, the English would soon prevail, due in part to the capture of Canonchet.

THE TIDE TURNS FOR PHILIP

The Indians' devastating string of early spring attacks had many English believing that they would soon be driven back to the sea. However, the English captured Canonchet in early April, 1676, depriving Philip of his most important military ally. The Narragansett sachem had been camping by the Pawtucket (Blackstone) River with a small group of warriors, when the English picked up his trail:

> Captain George Dennison...and Captain Avery...having raised forty-seven English with eighty (friendly) Indians, marched to Pawtucket in search of Canonchet... When Canonchet found that the enemy was close upon him he siezed his gun and sought to escape with a party of scouts at his heels. In crossing a small stream his foot slipped on a stone and he fell, wetting his gun. He was captured by (the English soldiers).... But though helpless and captive he was still a proud and unconquered chief.... When told that he might save his life by commanding his people to yield to the English, his resolution was not shaken by any threats or bribes. And when he was told of his sentence of death, he replied that he 'liked it well, that he should die before his heart was soft or he had spoken anything unworthy of himself.'

Tilton: 79-80

The fury of King Philip's War is still visible on this wooden door, removed from a 17th-century colonial home that once stood in Deerfield, Massachusetts. This fascinating relic – which has been on display at Deerfield's Memorial Hall – shows scars left by attacking Indians who attempted to hack through the door with tomahawks during an assault on Deerfield in 1675.

A contemporary but anonymous account of Canonchet's capture further conveys the majesty of this man (which the English naturally perceived as arrogance):

> (Canonchet's) carriage was strangely proud and lofty after he was taken; being examined why he did foment this war...he would make no other reply to any interrogatories, but this: that he was born a prince, and if princes came to speak to him he would answer; but none present being such, he thought himself obliged, in honor, to hold his tongue, and not hold discourse with such persons below his birth.... He told them that he would rather die than to continue under confinement.
>
> Anonymous, as quoted in Bliss: 100

Canonchet, chained with forty-three other captured Narragansetts, was taken to Stonington, Connecticut, where friendly Indians carried out his execution for the English. Canonchet was shot, and his body was drawn and quartered and burned. His head was sent to the council at Hartford as a grisly token of war.

The loss of Canonchet heralded the beginning of the end for Philip's cause. "No other leader could supply his combination of personal authority and strategic wisdom. Philip may have possessed considerable skills as diplomat...but it was to Canonchet that military leaders of the day gave the laurel for his generalship of the combined native forces (Bourne: 188)." The battlegrounds on which Canonchet and his warriors had wreaked terror and destruction would soon come under the control of the English.

ONE LAST ATTACK IN REHOBOTH

With the death of Canonchet, Rehoboth and surrounding south-eastern New England towns had already seen the worst they would of Indian violence. Still, the danger had not completely abated. In May of 1676, an Indian war party, returning from Wrentham, made an attack on the Woodcock garrison (in present-day Attleboro, Massachusetts, which back then was part of Rehoboth):

> His sons (i.e. Woodcock's) were at work in a cornfield near the house. The Indians, concealed in the (woods) adjoining the field, approached to its borders and fired upon them (killing one of them). The workmen fled to the garrison, leaving the dead body on the field. The Indians to gratify their spite against the family, cut off the son's head, stuck it on a long pole, which they set up on a hill at some distance in front of the house and in full view of the family, to aggravate their feelings as much as possible. From this time Woodcock swore never to make peace with the Indians. He ever after hunted them like wild beasts. He was a man of resolute and determined character; and tradition says, that not a few fell victim to his vengeance, and a sacrifice to the manes of his murdered son.
>
> Daggett, as quoted in Bliss: 102

THE CAPTURE AND DEATH OF KING PHILIP

The summer of 1676 was a tragic one for the Indians. With Canonchet dead, they had lost their military edge, and English forces encountered and captured many more Indians, a good number of whom were sold into slavery in the West Indies. To a great extent, the English prevailed because one of their military commanders, Benjamin Church, managed to break away from European notions of static warfare and used his woods sense and keen knowledge of the Indians to structure the tactics of his company:

Church's methods may have been unconventional in terms of traditional English warfare of the period, but he was as disciplined as he was inventive. In his account of the sorties carried out that summer of 1676, three tactics became recognizable: first, never to return from an area via the same route you took going in (thus he avoided the ambushes that Philip and others set for him); second, always to 'march thin and scatter;' that is, to proceed into a new area with each man at a fair distance from the next and without gathering in a 'heap together;' and third, to trust your native allies (friendly Indian scouts working with the English)...

Bourne: 198

By this time, Church and his troops were enjoying great success "in capturing and killing the enemy (rounding up fifty or sixty at a coup)...the area around Bridgewater and Taunton was particularly productive for his searchings and capturings, since this was a junction point for many of the native trails (Bourne: 198)."

Philip, who had earlier moved into New York in an unsuccessful attempt to win the support of the New York Ma04

hicans, was by now back in the area of his Mount Hope headquarters. Upon hearing of the capture (by Church) of his wife, Wootonekanuska, and his nine-year-old son, Philip is said to have cried, "My heart breaks; now I am ready to die" (the fate of Wootonekanuska and the boy remains uncertain; they were probably shipped off to the West Indies and put on the auction block as slaves).

Philip was zealously pursued by Church and his men:

From the pattern of his appearances, it seemed that

Philip was fleeing first here, now there, finally crossing the Taunton River and running toward his home at Mount Hope.... Elusive and clever as a fox...but he must have been exhausted. When one of his counselors suggested peace, Philip's mood was such that he killed the man with his own hand (with a hatchet).

It was the brother of the man Philip killed, Alderman by name, who stepped forth at the end of August and offered to take Benjamin Church directly to Philip's hide-out...Church listened to Alderman – 'who was a fellow of good sense and told his story handsomely' – and made his plans. He and his men would surround Philip's camp by night while expecting Philip to run to the other side, away from the English attack, just as Canonchet had. Church told the senior officer who had come to observe the operation: 'Sir, I have so placed (my men) that 'tis scarcely possible Philip should escape them.'

Although the first English soldier to fire on the sachem's camp did so prematurely, at early dawn, the situation developed precisely as Church had planned. Philip, hearing the exchanged shots, 'threw his petunk (pouch) and powder horn over his shoulder, catched up his gun, and ran as fast as he could scamper, without any more clothes than his small breeches and stockings.' He ran, as it happened, directly toward the spot where Alderman and the English soldier with whom he was paired were standing.

They let him come within shot, and (according to Church's account) 'the Englishman's gun missing fire, he bid the Indian (Alderman) fire away. And he did so to purpose, sent one musket ball through Philip's heart, and another not two inches from it. (Philip) fell upon his face in the mud and water, with his gun under him.

Bourne: 200-201

Philip's elderly sub-chief and war captain, Anawan, cried to the other Indians in Philip's band, "Iootash! Iootash!," meaning "Stand and fight." However, resistance was by now a lost cause, and the aged Anawan managed to escape with his companions through an unguarded part of the swamp.

Philip's body was most rudely treated by the English. He was "chopped in quarters, beheaded, and left unburied. The head and one hand were given to Alderman as a reward and, according to Church, he 'got many a penny' by showing the hand (Tilton: 81-82)." Soon, Philip's head was stuck on a pole at Plymouth, where it remained in view of passers-by for many decades. One preacher (Cotton Mather) "relished the sight and more than once 'took off the jaw from the skull of that blasphemous leviathan' (Bourne: 201)."

THE CAPTURE OF ANAWAN IN REHOBOTH

Anawan, elderly but with many survival skills, retreated with his band into Rehoboth, Massachusetts, to a strategic location comprised of a hill with a rock shelf, now designated "Anawan Rock:"

A sign by the wayside (Route 44) now indicates the spot. The rock is of conglomerate structure, running northeast and southwest about eighty feet, and from fifteen to twenty-five feet in height, of easy ascent on the west side, but on the southeast side broken somewhat precipitously with a fall of some six or eight feet. The difficulty of descent is often exaggerated, for one can easily get down by taking hold of the bushes on the edge of the rock.

The retreat was ideal, being close to the swamp (north end of Squannakonk Swamp) and on the steep side of the rock, with small trees growing about the base, but with space for mats to be spread for a resting place. It would hardly have been discovered by pursuers, unless piloted by Indian deserters or prisoners.

Tilton: 82-83

Captain Church went to work tracking Anawan and his companions:

Church followed the war captain's trail, tracking and questioning as he went north. Finally, at the beginning of September, he encountered an old man and his daughter who had recently come from Anawan's well-concealed camp. Enlisting them, Church and his small force hurried to the camp as the day ended. Then, from the top of the hill, he could see the campfires of the enemy being lit, and Anawan and his son preparing for sleep. Church urged his guides to clamber down the rope ahead of him with their packs full of supplies, and he prepared to follow immediately, in their shadow. When he reached the ground, however, Church was spotted at once, greeted with the astonished cry of 'Howoh!' ('who's there?'). But after he had identified himself and informed Anawan and his son how the situation lay, the surrender took place quite peacefully.

Bourne: 204

Anawan, despite his superior numbers, apparently realized that any resistance at this point in the war would be futile. To kill Church would only bring harsher treatment by the English. Believing it to be in the best interest of himself and his comrades, and with Church promising him fair treatment, he resigned himself to his fate.

Church spent the night with Anawan and his band, as it was now too dark for him to march his prisoners to town.

> While his men slept, Church, although greatly needing sleep himself, kept vigil with old Anawan. After a long conversation Anawan arose and walked a little way back from the company, and Captain Church began to suspect some ill design; but at length he returned with something in his hands...and he addressed Captain Church thus: '...you have killed Philip and conquered his country, for I believe that I and my companions are the last that war against the English, so suppose the war is ended by your means, and therefore these things belong to you.' He then presented him with what he said was Philip's (royal belts) with which he was wont to adorn himself when he sat in state. The first was a beautifully wrought belt nine inches in breadth, and of such length that when put upon the shoulders of Captain Church it reached his ankles. This was considered at that time of great value, being embroidered all over with wampum of various colors, curiously wrought into figures of birds, beasts, and flowers. The second belt was also of exquisite workmanship, with which Philip used to ornament his head, and from which flowed two flags which decorated his back. A third belt was a smaller one, with a star upon the end of it, which he wore upon his breast. All these were edged with red hair, which Anawan said was got in the country of the Mohawks. To these were added two horns of glazed powder and a red cloth blanket.
>
> Tilton: 84

The ultimate fate of Philip's exquisite wampum belts remains unknown. According to tradition, Church eventually gave the belts to Plymouth's Governor Winslow, who, in turn, supposedly presented them to Charles II of England. However, there is no conclusive evidence to indicate that belts definitely made it to England, or that they are present there now. There have been recent attempts to determine if they still exist (see Appendix C for a discussion of this interesting mystery).

Anawan and his comrades were brought to Plymouth. Despite Captain Church's promises of fair treatment, the old Wampanoag war captain was executed by the English, an act which, in the eyes of many historians, including this writer, fully disgraced the colonial government.

Though there would be a few more outbreaks of Indian hostilities, especially in northern areas like Maine and New Hampshire, the war, for all intents and purposes, had ended with the capture of Anawan.

> "When it was over, it was clear that Indians in New England were a dying race. They had made a final, heroic, passionate, futile bid for survival with self-respect. Although communities survived...rum, pestilence, and a failure of heart kept reducing their numbers."
>
> (LCHS: 35)

CONCLUSIONS

What about the modern historian who holds the colonists historically accountable for causing King Philip's War and for all the suffering and devastation that followed? Is he unfairly applying the moral standards and ethnic tolerance of his own 20th-century culture to 17th-century English New Englanders, whose actions were perhaps understandable in those less-enlightened times?

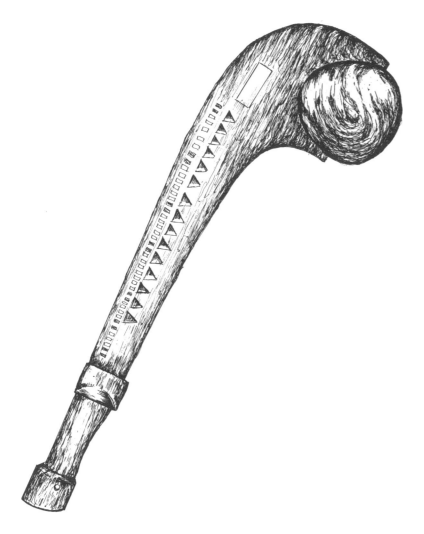

This beautiful Wampanoag war club – currently in the Fruitlands Museum Collection in Harvard, Massachusetts – is said to have belonged to King Philip. Unfortunately, King Philip's exquisite Wampum Belts have been lost to history, although attempts to locate them are still in progress (see Appendix C).

Considering the powerful, all-encompassing role of religion and Judeo-Christian ethics in the lives of 17th-century Puritan New Englanders, it seems difficult to excuse their actions on the basis of pre-enlightenment cultural ignorance or misunderstanding. Were they ignorant to the fact that paying the Indians roughly the equivalent of $2,500.00 for virtually all of the land contained in Massachusetts fell just a bit short of fairness? Did they not realize that by failing to adequately explain English property law to the Indians they were perhaps relying on misunderstanding and misinformation to negotiate land deals? Did they not understand the implications of plying a native full of unfamiliar alcohol and then asking him to sign a deed? Were they not aware that by claiming much more land than was agreed upon in original transactions they were, in fact, committing fraud and theft? More than anything else, it was these unfair dealings with the Indians that ultimately led to armed conflict.

It is not the author's intention to imply that all Englishmen dealt with the Indian population in these ways. Some colonists, especially the very first to arrive at Plymouth, dealt fairly with the local Indians. Yet, the plain truth is that a disturbingly large proportion of Englishmen did not.

Greed and deception have nothing to do with cultural or historical context. They have always been wrong, and man has always known them to be wrong. We can perhaps forgive the colonists for failing to appreciate an alternate culture. That failure might indeed be understandable given the less-enlightened nature of the period, a period in which the moral implications of racial prejudice and intolerance were not well-understood because they had yet to be explored within the public forum.

However, failing to understand or appreciate an alternate culture is quite different from taking ruthless advantage of it. We can be sure, based on what we know of the religious mood and teachings of their society, that the Puritans fully understood the moral implications of stealing and defrauding, of hypocrisy and of treating others in a completely different manner than they themselves would want to be treated (that last bit taken almost verbatim from the book on which the Puritans supposedly based their lives). However, the basic pattern was to spend Sundays in church condemning the religion of the Indian, and to spend the rest of the week stealing him blind.

King Philip's War had little to do with King Philip. It was about greed, hypocrisy, and insensitivity. These things caused the war, they fueled it, and they left an entire culture in ruins; in other words, the same old story.

Over three hundred years ago, a Puritan preacher, Cotton Mather, called the Indian a "savage." Ironically, this same man was known to relish the severed head of King Philip, stuck upon a pole at Plymouth. To Mather, that severed head symbolized an English triumph over "savagery." To any thoughtful person, that severed head symbolized that the English had merely managed to express a frightening savagery of their own. Little did the English know that the true "savages" – those most in need of confrontation – were the ones within themselves.

Like all wars, King Philip's War left many people in pain. People are still in pain. Acknowledged in our history books but not in our hearts, the war continues, to this very day, to hurt and wound the Native American community throughout the country. As long as we, as a culture, fail to acknowledge in our national holidays and remembrances the people at whose expense we became a society – as long as we fail to consider how we might pay fitting and substantive tribute to the Indian victims of our earlier holocausts – we, like Cotton Mather, are being less than honest with ourselves.

And, in the end, even fitting tribute is not enough. The right words will get us started, but actions must follow: "Native peoples should hold symbolic places of honor as the first North Americans. And, for having been deprived of most of what was once all their land by the people who came after them, they should be granted the necessary means to achieve their social and cultural goals (Waldman: 211)."

In reaching those goals, the Indians neither want nor need us to lead them. What they do want is for us to care enough to step aside, and to provide, as every nation should, whatever is necessary for a flourishing of cultural pluralism. Diversity does not have to mean division.

Until this happens, King Philip's War is still very much in progress.

Appendices

NATIVE NEW ENGLAND

The Long Journey

Appendix A

"Algonquin Myths, Legends and Ghost Lore"

.

Assembled and edited by Deborah Cahoon Didick
and Charles Robinson

Postscript by Deborah Cahoon Didick, Folklorist

Footnotes by Deborah Cahoon Didick,
Charles Robinson, Charles Leland

THE SILVER PIPE

(Wampanoag — Historic Period, 17th-century A.D.)

"King James of England, on hearing the goodness and virtues of Massasoit, once sent him a present of a silver pipe. The chieftain prized it highly as a gift from his 'white brother over the sea.' But one of his warriors did a deed of valor that so won his heart that he resolved to make him a present of the pipe as his choice treasure. The warrior, finding himself about to die, charged his squaw to put the silver pipe into his grave at the burial, but she, out of regard to the value of the treasure, hid it, and covered the grave without it.

One evening she went to the place where she had hidden the royal present, resolving to smoke from the pipe alone, and to hide it again. She put out her hand to take the pipe, but it moved away from her. Again, but it moved away, and again and again...(a) dead hand

was moving it. Then she bitterly repented of her disobedience, and promised to bury the pipe if she were able. At this resolution, the pipe lay still, and she opened the grave, fulfilled the warrior's command, and was enabled to smoke in peace of mind and conscience, we may hope, the rest of her days."

Butterworth, as quoted in Simmons: 124

Note by Deborah Cahoon Didick:

"Honoring the dead has always been a major cultural rule, carried out in many ritualistic forms which include prayer and praise, respectful treatment of the mortal remains, and inclusion into the grave of articles of special significance to the deceased.

Pharaoh and farmer, king and factory worker, saint and woodcarver have been laid to rest with treasured and symbolic articles. Even today, it would not seem strange to us for a musician to be buried with his drumsticks, a literate grandmother with her pen, a refugee with a sachet of earth from his homeland.

'Right of Sepulcher' is very much still a mandate; violation, to the present day, is punishable by law. Basic human respect decrees that the desecration of someone's grave is unthinkable. It is the right of every person to 'Rest in Peace.'"

OF THE WOMAN WHO LOVED A SERPENT WHO LIVED IN A LAKE

(Passamaquoddy, probably prehistoric in origin)

"Of old times. There was a very beautiful woman. She turned the heads of all the men. She married, and her husband died very soon after, but she immediately took another. Within a single year she had five husbands (who all died), and these were the cleverest and handsomest and bravest in the tribe. And then she married again.

This, the sixth, was such a silent man that he passed for a fool. But he was wiser than people thought. He came to believe, by thinking it over, that this woman had some strange secret. He resolved to find it out. So he watched her all the time. He kept his eye on her by night and by day.

It was summer, and she proposed to go into the woods to pick berries, and to camp there. By and by, when they were in the forest, she suggested that he should go to the spot where they intended to remain and build a wigwam. He said that he would do so. But he went a little way into the woods and watched her.

As soon as she believed that he was gone, she rose and walked rapidly onwards. He followed her, unseen. She went on, 'till, in a deep, wild place among the rocks, she came to a pond. She sat down and sang a song. A great foam, or froth, rose to the surface of the water. Then in the foam appeared the tail of a serpent. The creature was of immense size. The woman, who had laid aside all her garments, embraced the serpent, which twined around her, enveloping all her limbs and body in his folds. The husband watched it all. He now understood that, the venom of the serpent having entered the woman, she had saved her life by transferring it to the (other husbands), who died.

He went on to the camping ground and built a wigwam. He made up two beds. He built a fire. His wife came. She was earnest that there should only be a single bed. He sternly bade her lie by herself. She was afraid of him. She laid down and went to sleep. He arose three times during the night to replenish the fire. Everytime he called her, and there was no answer. In the morning he shook her. She was dead. She had died by the poison of the serpent. They sunk her in the pond where the snake lived."

Leland: 274

PETER SKY CHANGED TO A ROCK

(Scaticook, Historic Period)

This is the story of Peter Sky.... He used to go by a swamp that lay near a road. One dark night he and someone else went to town and got some whiskey. Then they came down that road until they reached a swamp. They took their whiskey down there and began to drink when they had found a nice place to sit on. Soon they fell to quarreling over their whiskey, and in the fight that followed Pete was killed. The other Indian got away and was never heard of again. But the next day some people coming by found Pete's body there and a rock with a hole in it close by. That rock was never noticed much by the Indians thereafter until one dark and foggy night, when some of them went down to the swamp on their way home to drink something they had bought. They heard noises from the rock, and one of them poured some of the goods into the hole. Immediately there was a voice from the rock. It called for more, and they kept on pouring whiskey in until the voice was the voice of a drunken man. That rock (which contained the soul of Pete) will 'holler' now on foggy nights if you pour whiskey into it."

Speck, as quoted in Simmons: 125

Note by Charles Robinson:

"This tale derives from Connecticut and seems to reflect the apprehension with which Native Americans in New England and elsewhere have regarded the white man's 'gift' of alcohol to the New World. The legend seems to warn both of the violence – even among friends – often associated with drunkeness, as well as the dangers of addiction (Pete's soul will forever cry out for passers-by to pour whiskey into his eternally thirsty and gaping mouth)."

THE GIRL-CHENOO

(Micmac, probably prehistoric in origin)

"Of the old time. Far up in the Saguenay River a branch turns off to the north, running back into the land of ice and snow. Ten families went up this stream one autumn in their canoes, to be gone all winter on a hunt. Among them was a beautiful girl, twenty years of age. A young man in the band wished her to become his wife, but she flatly refused him. Perhaps she did it in such a way as to wound his pride; certainly she roused all that was savage in him, and he gave up all his mind to revenge.

He was skilled in medicine, or in magic, so he went into the woods and gathered an herb which makes people insensible. Then stealing into the lodge when all were asleep, he held it to the girl's face, until she had inhaled the odor and could not be easily awakened. Going out he made a ball of snow, and returning placed it in the hollow of her neck, in front, just below the throat. Then he retired without being discovered.

When she awoke she was chilly, shivering, and sick. She refused to eat. This lasted long, and her parents became alarmed. They inquired what ailed her. She was ill-tempered; she said that nothing was the matter. One day, having been sent to the spring for water, she remained absent for so long that her mother went to seek her. Approaching unseen, she observed her greedily eating snow. And asking her what it meant, the daughter explained that she felt within a burning sensation, which the snow relieved. More than that, she craved the snow; the taste of it was pleasant to her.

After a few days she began to grow fierce, as though she wished to kill someone. At last she begged her parents to kill her. Hitherto she had loved them very much. Now she told them that unless they killed her she would certainly be their death. Her whole nature was being changed.

'How can we kill you?' her mother asked.

'You must shoot at me,' she replied, 'with seven arrows. And if you can kill me with seven shots all will be well. But if you cannot, I shall kill you.'

Seven men shot at her, as she sat in the wigwam. She was not bound. Every arrow struck her in the breast, but she sat firm and unmoved. Forty-nine times they pierced her; from time to time she looked up with an encouraging smile. When the last arrow struck she fell dead.

Then they burned the body, as she had directed. It was soon reduced to ashes, with the exception of the heart, which was of the hardest ice. This required much time to melt and break. At last all was over.

She had been brought under the power of an evil spirit; she was rapidly being changed into a Chenoo, a wild, fierce, unconquerable being. But she knew it all the while, and it was against her will. So she begged that she might be killed.

The Indians left the place; since that day none have ever returned to it. They feared lest some small part of the body might have remained unconsumed, and that from it another Chenoo would rise, capable of killing all whom she met."

Leland: 251-254

Note by Charles Leland:

"Among the Micmac, there was a detailed account of an Indian who went mad during the winter, ran away naked into the wilderness among the snows, and was unanimously declared to have turned into a Chenoo...The historical basis of the above tale, if it has any, may be the same – a case of lunacy; fiction and figure adding the incredible details."

ORIGIN OF NANTUCKET AND MARTHA'S VINEYARD
(Wampanoag, Historic Period, with prehistoric roots)

"The native Indians accounted for the islands of Nantucket and Martha's Vineyard by a mythical giant story which ran somewhat in this wise:

A great many moons ago there lived upon the Cape a giant named Maushop. One day he waded out into the sea to a great distance, for his legs were exceedingly long.... After a time his moccasins became full of sand, which made walking painful. Thereupon he emptied one, and the Island of Nantucket appeared above the surface of the water, while the sand which he poured from the other formed the island known as Martha's Vineyard. He lighted his pipe and volumes of smoke arose, obscuring the vision for miles around. Ever afterward, when fog appeared over the water, the Indians would exclaim, 'Here comes old Maushop's smoke.' "

Wing, as quoted in Simmons: 203

ANOTHER VERSION OF THE SAME

(Wampanoag, Historic Period, with prehistoric roots)

"Once upon a time there lived on the Atlantic coast a giant who used Cape Cod for his bed. One night, being restless, he tossed from side to side until his moccasins were filled with sand. This so enraged him that on rising in the morning he flung the offending moccasins from his feet, one alighting to form Martha's Vineyard, while the other became the since famous island of Nantucket."

TREE GHOSTS

(Narragansett, Historic Period)

"...it is said, that each of the spruce trees (in rural parts of Rhode Island) grows where a drop of Narragansett blood was shed. They will ever grow in South County, no matter how much civilization crowds them. It is said of one settler, that he decided to cut down every spruce tree on his 500 acres of Indian land because they haunted him, and he was killed in the attempt. He cut with such vengeance, when he heard the story that each spruce was the soul of a Narragansett killed by a white man, that a stately spruce which he set out to destroy, fell upon him and killed him.

They really do look, as they stand here, there, and everywhere throughout the Narragansett country, that they were souls of departed Red Folk."

Red Wing, as quoted in Simmons: 142

Note by Charles Robinson:

"The atrocious civilian massacre of the Great Swamp Fight in the seventeenth century is the likely basis for this legendary account, which seems to reflect unresolved cultural grief and anger of a perpetual sort."

ON THE TRACKS
(Niantic, Historic Period)

"Many years ago a tribe of Niantic Indians lived on the location of the town of Bradford, Rhode Island. In the early part of 1800, the New York, New Haven, and Hartford Line put a railroad from Stonington to Providence. There were a number of the tribe that lived there at that time. The railroad crossed a swamp between Westerly, (R.I.) and Bradford, which is known as White Dog Swamp. Many years ago an Indian and his dog were going home, taking a short cut by the railroad. They were killed by the train. Ever since on dark nights, the dog and the Indian have been seen there. The great white dog will be seen coming down the track cut in two, while the Indian beside him has no head. They go down the middle of the track as far as the brook and then disappear. Many have seen this and the story keeps many away from there on dark nights; but the swamp is still called the White Dog Swamp, to this day."

Lone Wolf, as quoted in Simmons: 140

NE HWAS, THE MERMAID
(Passamaquoddy, probably prehistoric in origin)

"A long time ago there was an Indian (who resided) with his wife and two daughters. They lived by a great lake, or the sea, and the mother told her girls never to go into the water there, for that, if they did, something would happen to them.

They, however, deceived her repeatedly. When swimming is prohibited it becomes delightful. The shore of this lake 'sands' away out or slopes to an island. One day they went to it, leaving their clothes on the beach. The parents missed them.

The father went to seek them. He saw them swimming far out, and called to them. The girls swam up to the sand, but could get no farther. Their father asked them why they could not. They cried that they had grown to be so heavy that it was impossible. They were all slimy; they grew to be snakes from below the waist. After sinking a few times in this strange slime they became very handsome, with long black hair and large, bright black eyes, with silver bands on their neck and arms.

When their father went to get their clothes, they began to sing the most exquisite tones:
  'Leave them there!'
  Hearing this, their mother began to weep, but the
  girls kept on:
  'It is all our own fault,
  But do not blame us;
  It will be none the worse for you.
  When you go in your canoe,
  Then you need not paddle;
  We shall carry it along!'

And so it was: when their parents went in the canoe, the girls carried it safely on everywhere.

One day some Indians saw the girl's clothes on the beach, and so looked out for the wearers. They found them in the water, and pursued them, and tried to capture them, but they were so slimy that it was impossible to take them, 'till one, catching hold of a mermaid by her long black hair, cut it off.

Then the girl began to rock the canoe, and threatened to upset it unless her hair was given to her again. The fellow who had played the trick at first refused, but as the mermaids, or snake-maids, promised that they should all be drowned unless this was done, the locks were restored. And the next day they were heard singing and were seen, and on her who had lost her hair it was all growing as long as ever."

Leland: 270-271

Note by Deborah Cahoon Didick:

"There is an association between water and the power of women. Water nymphs, sirens, Ladies of the Lake, mermaids – all are familiar cross-cultural images of the fluid, caressing, nurturing, protective, transforming nature of women. In the amniotic fluid of the mother's womb rests the power of the Goddess, for without this creative water the seed of human existence would never germinate. Whether it's Boticelli's 'Birth of Venus' from the sea on a scallop shell, the mother of Christ incanted as the 'Star of the Sea,' or the Passamaquoddy 'Ne Was' in the above tale, each conjures up an image which is at once familiar and comfortable."

WOMAN AFLOAT

(Wampanoag, Historic Period)

"At a certain spot near the ridge of the cliffs (of Gay Head) an old woman is sometimes seen floating through the air carrying a basket of fish."

Tantaquidgeon, as quoted in Simmons: 139

THE HAUNTED SWAMP

(Mohegan, Historic Period)

"(One) time Tantaquidgeon was riding home, and when he was passing the...swamp two dogs dashed from the bushes, and from their mouths they breathed fire. They ran along side, blowing flames at the horse's flanks until he had passed the swamp. A white horse's head has been seen lying there too, but when the person approached it, it (moved away). Women who have gone...near the swamp at night have felt hands grasping their skirts, and even herds of pigs have dashed out to terrify belated travelers at night. Some Indians claim to have felt hands grasping their feet as they went by."

Speck, as quoted in Simmons: 129

ORIGIN OF THE BLACK SNAKES

(Passamaquoddy, probably prehistoric in origin)

"Far away, very far in the north, there dwelt by the border of a great lake a man and his wife. They had no children, and the woman was very beautiful and passionate.

The lake was frozen over during the greater part of the year. One day when the woman cut away the ice, she saw in the water a bright pair of large eyes looking steadily at her. They charmed her so that she could not move. Then she distinguished a handsome face; it was that of a fine slender young man. He came out of the water. His eyes seemed brighter and more fascinating than ever; he glittered from head to foot; on his breast was a large shining silvery plate.

The woman learned that this was At-o-sis, the Serpent, but she returned his embraces and held conversation with him, and was so charmed with her lover that she not only met him more than once every day, but even went forth to see him in the night.

Her husband, noticing these frequent absences, asked her why she went forth so frequently. She replied, 'To get the fresh air.'

The weather grew warmer; the ice left the lake; grass and leaves were growing. Then the woman waited 'till her husband slept, and stole out from the man whom she kissed no more, to the lover whom she fondled and kissed more than ever.

At last the husband's suspicions being fairly aroused, he resolved to watch her. To do this he said that he would be absent for three days. But he returned at the end of the first day, and found that she was absent. As she came in he observed something like silvery scales on the logs. He asked what they were. She replied, 'brooches.'

He was still dissatisfied, and said that he would be gone for one day. He went to the top of a hill not far distant, whence he watched her. She went to the shore, and sat there. By and by there rose up out of the lake, at a distance, what seemed to be a brightly shining piece of ice. It came to the strand and rose from the water. It was a very tall and handsome man, dressed in silver. His wife clasped the bright stranger in her arms, kissing him again and again.

The husband was awed by this strange event. He went home, and

tried to persuade his wife to leave the place and return to her people. This she refused to do. He departed; he left her forever. But her father and mother came to find her. They found her there; they dwelt with her. Every day she brought them furs and meat. They asked her whence she got them. 'I have another husband,' she replied; 'one who suits me. The one I had was bad, and did not use me well. This one brings all the animals to me.' Then she sent them away with many presents, telling them not to return until the ice had formed; that was in autumn.

When they returned she had become white. She was with young, and soon gave birth to her offspring. It consisted of many serpents. The parents went home. As they departed she said to them, 'When you come again you may see me, but you will not know me.'

Years later some hunters, roaming that way, remembered the tale, and looked for the wigwam. It was there, but no one was in it. But all the woods about the place were full of great black snakes, which would rise up like a human being and look one in the face, then glide away without doing any harm."

Leland: 278-279

CAPTAIN KIDD AND THE PIRATES
(Mohegan, Historic Period)

"In the days of Captain Kidd he and other buccaneers used to come up the Thames River (of Connecticut) in their boats and lie to during the periods of pursuit. Up there among the Indians they could pass the time pleasantly, and also find secluded regions wherein to bury their booty. So the Mohegans have some tales of these visits from the pirates which have furnished the motive for many nightly excursions to dreamt-of spots where treasure is thought to exist. Until this day futile attempts are made to lay hands on some of the gold that is said to be buried along the river shores.

One night two Mohegans, having dreamed of a certain spot where Kidd's money was buried, went down to the river with spades. They began their trench, and soon had the good fortune to disclose the top of a great iron box with a ring in it. Their surprise was so great that one of them said, 'Here it is!' At that moment a tremendous black dog appeared at the rim of the pit and growled. At the same moment the chest vanished. The men were so terrified that they never tried to find the place again.

Sometimes the animal, instead of being a dog, is a pig, and it has even been reported as a terrible-looking man with long robes and clotted hair. It is explained by the belief that Kidd, when he buried his loot, always killed some animal or man and threw him into the pit in order that his spirit might guard the pot."

Speck, as quoted in Simmons: 164

FRAGMENT OF AN ANCIENT SONG
(Micmac, prehistoric. Only a small part survives)

"There was a woman, long, long ago,
She came out of a hole.
In it dead people were buried.
She made her house in a tree;
She was dressed in leaves,
All long ago.
When she walked among the dry leaves
Her feet were so covered
The feet were invisible.
She walked through the woods,
Singing all the time,
'I want company; I am lonesome!'
A wild man heard her:
From afar over the lakes and mountains
He came to her.

She saw him; she was afraid;
She tried to flee away,
For he was covered with the rainbow;
Color and light were his garments.
She ran, and he pursued rapidly;
He chased her to the foot of a mountain.
He spoke in a strange language;
She could not understand him at first.
He would make her tell where she dwelt.
They married; they had two children.
One of them was a boy;
He was blind from his birth,
But he frightened his mother by his sight.
He could tell her what was coming,
What was coming from afar.
What was near he could not see.
He could see the bear and the moose
Far away beyond the mountains;
He could see through everything."

Leland: 310

Note by Charles Robinson:

"*Because this remarkable material is so ancient and fragmentary, it is difficult for us to determine the precise meaning of its unusual characters. Perhaps the tale celebrates some popular medicine man, or shaman, who may have once actually lived. The peculiar 'sight' attributed to the 'blind' boy near the end of the song is characteristic of shamanism – an art whose practitioner's success depended upon his or her ability to see into the invisible spirit world – to view things that other, more ordinary mortals never could.*"

THE MOURNFUL MYSTERY OF
THE PARTRIDGE WITCH

(Micmac, probably prehistoric)

"Of the olden time. Two brothers went hunting in the autumn, and (they ventured) as far as the head waters of the Penobscot, where they remained all winter. But in March their snow-shoes gave out, as did their moccasins, and they wished that a woman was there to mend them.

When the younger brother returned first to the lodge, the next day, – which he generally did to get it ready for the elder, – he was astonished to find that someone had been there before him, and that, too, in the housekeeping. For garments had been mended, the place cleaned and swept, a fire built, and the pot was boiling. He said nothing of this to his brother; but returning the next day at the same time, found that all had been attended to, as at first. And again he said nothing: but in the morning, when he went forth to hunt, he did but go a little way, and, returning, watched, from a hidden place, the door. And there came a beautiful and graceful girl, well attired, who entered the wigwam. And he, stepping softly, looking through a hole in the hut, saw her very busy with his housekeeping.

Then he entered, and she seemed to be greatly alarmed and confused; but he calmed her, and they soon became good friends, sporting together very happily all day long like children, for indeed they were both young.

When the sun's height was little and his shadows long, the girl said, 'I must go now. I hear your brother coming, and I fear him. But I will return tomorrow. Addio!' So she went, and the elder brother knew nothing of what had happened. The next day she came again, and once more they played in sunshine and shadow until evening;

but ere she went he sought to persuade her to remain always. And she, as if in doubt, answered, 'Tell thy brother all, and it may be that I will stay and serve ye both. For I can make the snow-shoes and moccasins which ye so much need, and also canoes.' Then she departed with the day, and the elder, returning, heard from his brother all that had happened, and said, 'Truly, I should be glad to have someone here to take care of the wigwam and make snow-shoes.'

So she came in the morning, and hearing from the younger that his brother had consented to her coming was very glad, and went away, as in haste. But she returned about noon, drawing a toboggin (sled) piled up with garments and arms, for she was a huntress. Indeed, she could do all things as few women could, whether it were cooking, needlework, or making all that men need. And the winter passed very pleasantly, until the snow grew soft, and it was time for them to return. 'Till she came they had little luck in hunting, but since her coming all had gone well with them, and now they had a wonderful quantity of furs.

Then they returned in the canoe, going down the river to their village. But as they came near it the girl grew sad, for she had thrown out her soul to their home, though they knew it not, by meelahbigive (clairvoyance, or state of vision). And suddenly she said, as they came to a point of land, 'Here I must leave. I can go no farther. Say nothing of me to your parents, for your father would have but little love for me.' And the young men sought to persuade her, but she only answered sorrowfully 'It cannot be.' So they came home with their furs, and the elder was so proud of their luck and their strange adventure that he could not hold his peace, but told all.

Then his father was very angry, and said, 'All my life I have feared this. Know that this woman was a devil of the woods, a witch of the Mitche-hant, a sister of the Oonahgamess (goblins and ghosts)....'

And he spoke so earnestly and so long of this thing that they were afraid, and the elder, being persuaded by the sire, went forth to slay her, and the younger followed him afar. So they sought her by the stream, and found her bathing, and, seeing them, she ran up a little hill. And, as she ran, the elder shot an arrow at her. Then there was a strange flurry about her, a fluttering of scattered feathers, and they saw her fly away as a partridge. Returning, they told all this to their father, who said, 'You did well. I know all about these female devils who seek to destroy men...'

But the younger could not forget her, and longed to see her again; so one day he went into the woods, and there he indeed found her, and she was as kind as before. Then he said, 'Truly it was not by my goodwill that my brother shot at you.' And she answered, 'Well do I know that, and that it was all by your father; yet I blame him not, for this is an affair of N'karnayoo, the days of old; and even yet it is not at an end, and the greatest is to come. But let the day be only a day unto itself; the things of tomorrow are for tomorrow, and those of yesterday are departed.' So they forgot their troubles, and played together merrily all day long in the woods and in the open places, and told stories of old times 'till sunset. And as the Kah-kah-goos (crow) went to his tree, the boy said, 'I must return'; and she replied, 'Whenever you would see me, come to the woods. And remember what I say. Do not marry anyone else. For your father wishes you to do so, and he will speak of it to you soon. Yet it is for your sake only that I say this.' Then she told him word by word all that his father had said; but he was not astonished, for now he knew that she was not as other women; but he cared not. And he grew brave and bold, and then he was above all things. And when she told him that if he should marry another he would surely die, it was as nothing to him.

Then returning, the first thing his father said was, 'My son, I have provided a wife for you, and the wedding must be at once.' And he said, 'It is well. Let it be so.' Then the bride came. For four days they held the wedding dance; four days they feasted. But on the last day he said, 'This is the end of it all,' and he laid himself down on a white bear-skin rug, and a great sickness came upon him, and when they brought the bride to him he was dead."

Leland: 295-298

Note by Charles Leland:

"In this strange story...there is an element of mystery and destiny.... The family secret, touched on but never explained, which ends in such a death, is, speaking from an artistic point of view, very skillfully managed...(Characteristic of this type of story) is the growth in the hero, when he knows the worst to come, of that will, or stoicism, or complete indifference to fate, which the Indians regard as equivalent to attaining m'teoulin, or magic power. When a man has in him such courage that nothing earthly can do more than increase it, he has attained to what is in one sense at least Nirvana. From an Algonquin point of view the plot is perfect."

POSTSCRIPT

Deborah Cahoon Didick, Folklorist

Native American legends like the ones presented above have a universal appeal. Their lessons are noble and free, gentle yet firm. Their imagery reflects the power of nature which is at once beautiful and terrifying. The wilderness of fire, water, mountains, and animals; the dimensions of male prowess and female strength; the complexities of good and evil, beauty and ugliness, truth and foolishness, life and death...all of these things comprise the colors of folklore's palette.

Folklore, itself, is the study of the "spirit" of the people. Drawing from the deep well of myths, folktales, and legends that have survived the centuries, we are provided with an intimate window onto areas of human experience which normally aren't covered in the history books. People have always sought to know "why," to explain things not understood. Folklore is, then, a dynamic dialogue between humanity and the forces of nature (both physical and metaphysical).

As you read through the above stories, you perhaps noticed certain familiar archetypes relating to life, death, creation, destruction, wise men, and strong women. For all our cultural differences, reading these tales – which derive from an ancient culture distinctly different from our own – we nonetheless find them somehow familiar. It is only the particular external forms that our different; the themes strike recognizable chords. Consider, if you will, these cultural fragments as pieces of multi-colored glass in an anthropological kaleidoscope: always the same basic view, yet always shifting into new patterns.

REFERENCES, BOTH CITED AND CONSULTED, FOR APPENDIX A

Bettelheim, Bruno. *The Uses Of Enchantment: The Meaning And Importance Of Fairy Tales*, New York: Random House, 1977.

Campbell, Joseph. *The Power of Myth*, New York: Doubleday, 1988.

Erdoes, Richard. *American Indian Myths And Legends*, New York: Pantheon, 1984.

Graves, Robert. *The White Goddess*, New York: Farrar & Giroux, 1976.

Jung, Carl G. *Man And His Symbols*, New York: Doubleday, 1964.

Leland, Charles. *Algonquin Legends*, Boston: Dover Publishing, 1992.

Robinson, Charles. *Asleep Beneath The Meadows: The Indian Archaeology Of Rehoboth, Massachusetts*, Providence: Universal Press, 1992.

Russell, Howard S. *Indian New England Before The Mayflower* Princeton: University Press Of New England, 1980.

Simmons, William S. *Spirit Of The New England Tribes: Indian History And Folklore*, Princeton: University Press Of New England, 1986.

Appendix B

Algonquin Food Preparation and Recipes

Research and Compilation by Phyllis Dupere

CHIPPEWA BANNOCK

2 cups cornmeal
$\frac{1}{4}$ cup berries (blueberries, cranberries, or strawberries)
$\frac{3}{4}$ cup water
Honey to taste
$\frac{1}{4}$ cup sunflower seed oil
Additional oil for frying

Mix together the first five ingredients. Drop batter by the tablespoon into a large frying pan which has been greased liberally. Flatten into cakes. Cook, turning once, until golden on each side. (Serves 6).

BAKED SQUIRREL

1 squirrel, skinned (from gourmet shop, not wild)
$\frac{1}{2}$ cup milk
$\frac{1}{2}$ cup chopped onion

Section squirrel and flour. Brown in skillet. Place in covered baking dish. Cover with milk and onions. Bake until tender.

NUT BUTTER

1 cup shelled dried nuts or seeds
2 teaspoons maple syrup or honey

Grind 1 cup of dried seeds (or nuts) into a paste, using a mortar and pestle. Add honey or maple syrup to sweeten.

Use as topping on breads and cakes. Serve with fresh fruits or on vegetables.

Keep refrigerated. (Makes 1 cup).

SUMMER SQUASH SOUP

2 medium yellow squash, diced
3 onions
1 quart water
1 tablespoon sunflower oil
1 tablespoon honey
1 tablespoon chopped dillweed
Sunflower seeds (shelled) as garnish

In a large covered pot, simmer the squash, onions, honey, and oil in the water until the squash is tender. Mash to a smooth puree and add dillweed. Simmer an additional 5 minutes. Serve with garnish. (Serves 8).

TURTLE SOUP

1 pound turtle meat (from gourmet shop)
3 scallions, chopped
3 quarts water
1 tablespoon chopped fresh dillweed

Combine all ingredients in a large pot and simmer for 2 hours. Remove the turtle meat, cool slightly, and dice meat into bite-size pieces. Return the meat to the pot. Add more water, if necessary. Cook at low heat for another half-hour or until tender. (Serves 6).

STEWED CHERRIES

1 quart black cherries, stoned
1 cup maple syrup
1 cup cider

Simmer the cherries, maple syrup, and cider in a large covered crock – stirring occasionally – for 30 minutes.

CLAMBAKE

24 quahogs in the shell, washed
36 clams in the shell, washed
36 mussels in the shell, washed
6 1-1½ pound lobsters
6 ears of corn in husks
6 medium unpeeled potatoes, washed
6 onions
2 quarts water

In the bottom of a very deep, large pot, place the quahogs. Arrange the corn and lobsters on top of the quahogs. Add mussels and clams to fill in gaps. On top, place the potatoes and onions. Pour water over all. Cover and bring to a boil. Once boiling, reduce heat to a simmer and continue cooking for one hour or until potatoes are tender. (Serves 6).

GRAPE BUTTER

2 pounds grapes
Honey

Stem and wash the grapes. Place the grapes, covered with water, in a large pot and bring to a boil. Stirring continuously, simmer until the grape skins pop. Pour off the grape juice. It can be sweetened with honey to taste, and used as a beverage.

Sieve the remaining grape pulp to remove the seeds, and puree. Add an equal measure of honey, mixing puree and honey in a bean-pot. Bake in a 325° F oven for 3 hours, stirring occasionally.

Spread on bread or cake. Keep refrigerated.

CRANBERRY SAUCE

8 cups cranberries
1 cup maple syrup
1 cup chopped walnuts
½ cup cider
2 apples peeled, cored, and sliced

Place all the ingredients in a large kettle. Cover and bring to a boil. Simmer until the skins of the cranberries pop, about 30 minutes. Cool slightly. Serve either warm or cold. Excellent with turkey or other fowl. (Yields 1 quart).

CRANBERRY AND WALNUT SAUCE

1 pound cranberries
2 cups water
½ pound chopped walnut meats
1 cup maple syrup
2 tablespoons cornstarch mixed with enough water to make a thick paste

Place cranberries and water in a covered pot, bring it to a boil, lower heat, and cook until the cranberry skins pop. Add the walnuts and maple syrup. Cook at low heat for another ten minutes, then thicken with cornstarch paste, stirring until all is blended. Serve either hot or chilled with any fowl or game. (Makes 3 cups).

SUCCOTASH

1 chopped onion
1 chopped pepper
2 cups fresh corn, cut from ears
2 cups fresh lima beans, shelled
1 cup water
2 tablespoons of walnut butter

Cook ingredients together in a large covered pot at a simmer for 25 minutes. Serve hot as an accompaniment to meat dishes. (Serves 8).

WALNUT AND PUMPKIN SOUP

1 pumpkin (10 inches in diameter)
1 cup chopped walnuts
1 quart water
Maple syrup to taste
Roasted pumpkin seeds as garnish

Wash pumpkin. Roast it in a 325° F oven for 1 hour (or until flesh is tender). Remove from oven. Cool. Cut open the pumpkin and spoon out the seeds. Save them for roasting. Scoop out the pumpkin meat and place into a large saucepan. Add water, maple syrup, and walnuts until a desired consistency is attained. Cover, simmer an additional 5 minutes. Serve garnished with pumpkin seeds. (Serves 6).

CHAMOMILE TEA

1 teaspoon fresh or dried chamomile blossoms
1 cup boiling water

Place blossoms in cup and cover with boiling water. Allow to steep for 5 minutes. (Serves 1).

This soothing tea can be used as a hair rinse. As a soil sweetener, it benefits plant roots.

BAKED STUFFED KUTA SQUASH

1 large kuta squash
2 tablespoons sunflower oil
4 medium onions, peeled and chopped
1 pound mushrooms, sliced

Preheat oven to 375°. In a large pan, bring water to a boil. Cut the top off Kuta; scoop out the seeds. Put squash in boiling water and parboil for three minutes. Lift squash out of water and drain. Cool slightly. In a frying pan, add oil and onions. Fry until softened. Stir in mushrooms and fry two minutes more. Scoop out the flesh from the squash and mix with the vegetable mixture. Place this mixture into squash shell. Arrange the stuffed Kuta in a greased baking dish. Bake for 10-15 minutes or until the inside is hot. (Serves 4).

PEMMICAN

$\frac{1}{2}$ cup raisins
$\frac{1}{2}$ cup hickory nuts
$\frac{1}{2}$ cup dried apples
$\frac{1}{2}$ cup dried pumpkin
$\frac{1}{2}$ cup cornmeal
$\frac{1}{2}$ cup honey

Dry the cornmeal by placing it on a cookie sheet in a warm oven for 20-30 minutes. Check and stir every 10 minutes. With a knife, chop fruits and nuts, and add cornmeal and honey. Mix well and press into serving size patties. Use as a high energy trail mix. (Serves 12).

BARBECUED RABBIT

Skin and split rabbit (from gourmet shop, not wild). Rub generously with oil and barbecue over charcoal, turning often. Rabbit may be basted with seasoned oil as it is cooking. Cook until tender. Rabbit meat should be well done.

ROAST DUCK WITH STUFFING

1 4-5 pound duck, dressed
1 cup cider for basting

Stuffing:
Giblets
1 cup grapes
1 cup chopped mushrooms
4 apples, cored and quartered
1 cup chopped walnuts

4 whole potatoes
4 whole onions

Simmer the giblets in 2 cups of water for 45 minutes. Remove giblets, chop, and return to the stock. Add mushrooms, apples, grapes, and walnuts. Mix thoroughly.

Clean the duck. Stuff cavity and truss. Prick the skin with a sharp fork to allow fat to run off. Place duck on a rack in a roasting pan. Place potatoes and onions around the bird during final hour of cooking.

Roast for $3\frac{1}{2}$ hours at 325°. Prick the skin and baste with cider every 30 minutes. The duck is done when the meat on the drumstick feels soft or when the drumstick breaks away from the body. (Serves 4).

BROILED SCROD

1 large scrod, gutted
$\frac{1}{4}$ cup sunflower seed oil
1 teaspoon dillseed

Clean the scrod. Remove head, backbone, and tail. In a greased pan, place the fish, flesh side up. Coat with oil. Sprinkle with dill. Broil for 20 minutes or until browned. Serve hot. Garnish with greens. (Serves 4).

SUNFLOWER SEED SOUP

2 cups sunflower seeds, shelled
3 cups scallions
6 cups water
1 teaspoon chopped fresh dillweed

Simmer all ingredients in a large pot, covered, for 40 minutes. Stir occasionally. Serve hot. (Serves 6).

SUNFLOWER SEED CAKES

2 cups shelled sunflower seeds
$2\frac{1}{2}$ cups water
4 tablespoons fine cornmeal
$1\frac{1}{2}$ teaspoons maple syrup
Oil for frying

In a heavy, covered saucepan, simmer the seeds in the water for an hour. Drain well. Grind seeds. Combine the cornmeal, maple syrup, and ground seeds to make a stiff dough. Shape into flat cakes about 3 inches in diameter.

Brown the sunflower cakes in hot oil – on both sides – in a heavy skillet. Drain on absorbent paper. Serve hot. (Serves 5).

Appendix C

The Mystery Of King Philip's Lost Wampum Belts

NOTE: The following article originally appeared in the *Providence Journal-Bulletin* on March 15, 1996 and is reproduced here with permission:

Searching For Their Past

Three wampum belts – the only artifacts the Wampanoags used to record their history – were lost to the English at the end of King Philip's War. The question is, do they still exist?

By Pia Sarkar, *Providence Journal-Bulletin* Staff Writer

REHOBOTH – To the ordinary eye, they are pieces of fabric stitched with beads. But to the Wampanoag Nation, they tell stories of war and famine, feasts and celebrations. They describe events crucial to Wampanoag culture. And they are part of a history that has been missing for more than 300 years.

The three wampum belts – upon which the Wampanoags stitched scenes from their past – were lost to the English at the end of King Philip's War in 1676.

Attempts to recover the belts have ended in disappointment. But State Representative Phil Travis (D-Rehoboth) has resurrected efforts in hopes that the artifacts will finally be returned to their rightful owners.

"The bottom line is that the Native Americans have been mistreated," he said. "This is a physical history that has been lost to them."

Travis sponsored a resolution adopted by the State House of Representatives last March asking the British government to locate the missing belts. During a vacation in England, he delivered the resolution to the Commonwealth and Foreign Office at Whitehall in London.

The British government replied to Travis that "given the uncertainty over what became of them in 1676, and the length of time that has passed since then, the prospect for finding evidence about the belts is not good."

The resolution now sits in the foreign office, with little sign of activity. Progress in locating the belts has been slow at best, but Travis remains patient.

"They're still accountable somewhere," he said.

"At least we have people looking and thinking."

The investigation was originally prompted by Robert Sharples, member and former chairman of the Rehoboth Historical Commission. Sharples said his interest was stirred while working with Maurice Robbins, a former Massachusetts State Archaeologist who had been researching the belts' history for many years.

In 1990, after Robbins died, Sharples took over the project. "I figured as a tribute to him, I'd try to find these belts," he said.

Sharples sent a letter to Prince Charles requesting help from the British government, but he received no response.

"I'm very pleased that Rep. Travis is following this up," said Russell Peters, President of the Mashpee Wampanoag Indian Tribal Council.

He said at least two other groups from the Mashpee Wampanoags have gone to England to retrieve the belts but have come back empty-handed. "It's like searching for a needle in a haystack," Peters said.

One of the wampum belts is said to be nine inches wide, made of black leather and adorned with beaded decorations in the form of birds, beasts, and flowers, according to Robbin's documented research.

Another belt – which Metacomet, the Indian chief known as King Philip, wore around his head – had two flags that hung down his back. The third one was a small belt with a pewter star on the end, which King Philip used to hang upon his breast. All three were edged with red moose hair in a design depicting the Totem of the Wolf, the emblem of the Wampanoag Indian Federation.

Author Charles Turek Robinson, who writes about the wampum belts in his book *Asleep Beneath The Meadows: The Indian Archaeology of Rehoboth, Massachusetts*, describes them as "culturally urgent relics."

Once a year, at Nikommosachmiawene – a feast during which the council would meet – tribal warriors would sit in a ring about a fire and read from the beaded belts.

"They were the means by which the tribe's history would be related to younger generations," Robinson said. The belts were appended annually, their lengths growing longer and longer over time.

"Our people didn't do a lot of writing in that period of time," Peters adds. "It was generally oral tradition and the beads (belts) helped in the recollection of certain events."

They were also used in trading and presented as gifts to other tribes, Peters said. "They performed a very important function."

Specifics a Mystery

Each member of the council would interpret the belts as they were passed around the circle. Some of the history typically included military victories and defeats, famines and sicknesses, births and marriages.

But very few specifics are known about the recordings on the belts. "No modern-day researchers have seen the belts," Robinson said.

What is known is that King Philip gave the belts to his war captain, Anawan, for safe-keeping. The belts were normally passed down on a hereditary basis, but King Philip's son was being held

...t the time; (therefore), the artifacts were

.ng Philip's War, Anawan surrendered the belts to
. Church at what is now known as Anawan Rock in

.ter, Anawan was marched to Plymouth and executed,
.omises made by Church to the contrary, Robinson said.

.nurch had recorded in his diary that Anawan had voluntarily given up the belts, but Robinson thinks the events occurred much differently.

"It's very hard to believe that Anawan would treat these belts so lightly," he said, noting their great spiritual significance and speculating that the artifacts were forcibly taken.

Records show that Church had handed the belts to Governor Winslow of Plymouth Colony, who then entrusted them to his brother-in-law, Waldergrave Pelham, with instructions to transfer them to King Charles II at Whitehall in England.

Three years later, King Charles II sent a letter back to Governor Winslow stating that he never received the belts, Robinson said.

Do They Exist?

Although no further records of the belts have been uncovered, Robinson has offered some possibilities as to their whereabouts.

One is that Pelham pulled the wampum beads – which were at the time a primary source of currency – off the belts and used them to pay off his debts.

Another is that the ship on which the belts were carried was pirated or sunk. Or perhaps Charles II, not fully understanding the belts' significance, simply discarded them.

The last possibility is that the belts are in a depository in England and have yet to be uncovered. But, Robinson said, "I don't think that's likely."

"The only record we do have of these belts is that they were handled carelessly," he said. "They are likely the casualty of cultural indifference."

Peters, however, is a little more optimistic. "The English don't lose such things. We believe they are still there."

Courtesy of John Monaghan and the Providence Journal-Bulletin

Note by Charles Robinson:

Since the appearance of the above Providence Journal-Bulletin article – for which I was interviewed in February of 1996 – certain English officials, at the prompting of Representative Travis, have apparently stepped up their efforts to determine the possible whereabouts of the belts in Britain. As of this writing, they have enjoyed no success and still possess no substantive leads, furthering my suspicions that the magnificent wampum belts of King Philip remain lost to history.

Appendix D

Native New England Medicinals

The following list, which delineates regional trees, shrubs, and herbs that were utilized as medicinals by various New England tribes, by no means represents a complete listing of all such herbaceous medicines used in New England, but rather is limited to some of the more common ones.

Readers, of course, are cautioned not to eat, drink, or otherwise utilize any of the following trees, shrubs, or herbaceous plants except upon the advise of a medical doctor experienced in the application of herbal medicinals.

Knowledge and/or specific utilization of various herbaceous remedies varied considerably from tribe to tribe.

Common Name	Botanical Name	Bodily Influence
Alder	Alnus rugosa (DuRoi) Spreng	Astringent, Carthartic
Balsam Fir	Abies balsamea (L.) Mil	Expectorant, Stimulant
Blackberry	Rubus allegheniensis Porter	Astringent, Tonic
Bloodroot	Sanguinaria canedensis L.	Emetic, Diuretic,
Boneset	Eupatorium perfoliatum L.	Stimulant, Aperient
Butter Nut	Juglans cinerea L.	Carthartic, Vermifuge
Cedar, Red	Juniperus virginiana L.	Medicinal (various)
Cherry, Red	Prunus virginiana L.	Sedative, Tonic
Cranberry	Vaccinium macrocarpen Ait.	Uncertain
Ginseng	Panax quinquefolius L.	Stimulant, Demulcent
Hemlock	Tsuga anadensis (L.) Carr.	Uncertain
Hops	Humulus Lupulus L.	Sedative, Diuretic
Hemp	Apocynum cannabinum	Diverse

Common Name	Botanical Name	Bodily Influence
Juniper	Juniperus communis L	Stimulant, Diuretic
Lady's Slipper	Cypripedium reginae Walt.	Antiperiodic, Nervine
Lobelia,	See "Indian Tobacco", below	
"Indian Tobacco"	Lobelia inflata L.	Stimulant, Relaxant
Milkweed	Asclepias syriaca L.	Diaphoretic, Other
Oak, Red	Quercus rubra L.	Antiseptic, Astringent
Partridge Berry	Mitchella repens L.	Parturient, Tonic
Pennyroyal	Hedeoma pulegiodis L.	Corrective, Nervine
Pyrola	Pyrolla elliptica Nutt.	Antispasmodic, Tonic
Rasberry, Red	Rubus idaeus L.	Stimulant, Tonic
Rattlesnake Root	Polygala Senega L.	Snakebite antidote
Sarsaparilla	Aralia nudicaulus L.	Alternative, Demulcent
Skunk Cabbage	Symplocarpus foetidus Nutt.	Stimulant, Expectorant
Solomon's Seal	Polygonatum canaliculatum	Astringent, Demulcent
Sumac	Rhus glabra L.	Astringent, Tonic
Sweet Flag	Acorus Calamus L	Aromatic, Stomachic
Tobacco	Nicotinia rustica L.	Stimulant, Analgesic
Wintergreen	See "Pyrola"	See "Pyrola"

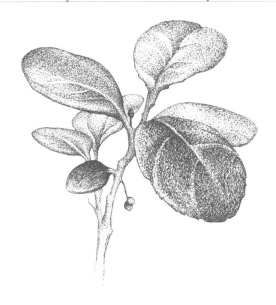

Selected References

Bliss, Leonard, Jr. *The History of Rehoboth*. Boston: Otis, Blanders, and Company, 1836.

Blumenthal, Walter H. *American Indians Dispossesed*. Philadelphia: G. McManus & Co., 1955.

Bonfonti, Leo. *Biographies and Legends of the New England Indians Volume II*. Wakefield, MA: Pride Publications, 1970.

Braun, Esther. Braun David. *The First Peoples of the Northeast*. Lincoln, MA: The Lincoln Historical Society, 1994.

Bourne, Russell. *The Red King's Rebellion*. New York: Atheneum, 1990.

Bowen, Richard Lebaron. *Early Rehoboth Volume III*. Rehoboth, MA: Privately Printed, 1948.

Bradford, William. *History of Plymouth Plantation*. Printed from the original manuscript under direction of the Secretary of the Commonwealth. Boston: Wright and Potter, 1898.

Butler, Eva L. *"Sweat Houses in the Southern New England Area."* **The Bulletin Of The Massachusetts Archaeological Society,** October, 1945; 11-15.

Cahill, Robert E. *Viking And Indian Wars*. Peabody, MA: Chandler-Smith Publishing, 1986.

Canby, Thomas Y. *"The Search for the First Americans."* **National Geographic,** 156 (September, 1979, no. 3); 330-363.

Dyer, E. Otis. *"Early Rehoboth Garrison Houses."* **The Rehoboth Reporter,** January, 1991; 18-19.

Fagan, Brian. *Archaeology: A Brief Introduction*. New York: Harper Collins, 1991.

Floyd, Candace. *The History of New England*. New York: Portland House, 1990.

Fowler, William S. *"Interpretation of the Evidence."* **The Bulletin of the Massachusetts Archaeological Society**- April, 1953; 98-99.

Fowler, William S. *"Eating Practices in Aboriginal New England."* **The Bulletin of the Massachusetts Archaeological Society** April/July, 1975; 6-11.

Gowlett, John. *Ascent To Civilization: The Archaeology of Early Man*. London: William, Collins, Sons & Co., 1984.

Gramley, R.M. *The Adkins Site: A Paleo-Indian Habitation and Associated Stone Structure*. Persimmon Press Monographs In Archaeology, 1988.

Hoffman, Curtis R. *A Handbook of Artifacts from Southern New England*. Massachusetts Archaeological Society Special Books and Publications, 1991.

Hoffman, Curtis R. *People of the Freshwater Lake: A Prehistory of Westborough, Massachusetts*. New York: Peter Lang, 1990.

Hutchens, Alma R. *Indian Herbalogy of North America.* Boston: Shamgahla, 1991.

Kopper, Philip. *The Smithsonian Book of the North American Indian.* Smithsonian Institution, 1988.

Leland, Charles. *The Algonquin Legends of New England.* Boston: Houghton, Mifflin and Co., 1884.

Luedke, Barbara. *The Camp at the Bend in the River.* Massachusetts Historical Commission Special Publication. December, 1995.

Little Compton Historical Society. Reprint of Benjamin Church's *Diary of King Philip's War.* Chester: The Pequot Press, 1975.

Mason, Estelle. *"Titicut Child of the Earth."* **Bulletin of the Massachusetts Archaeological Society**- October, 1971 to January, 1972; 10-12.

Massachusetts Historical Commission. **Historical and Archaeological Resources of the Boston Area.** Massachusetts Historical Commission Special Publication, January, 1982.

Ritchie, William A. *The Archaeology of New York State.* Harrison, NY: Harbor Hill Books, 1980.

Robbins, Maurice. *Wapanucket No. 6: An Archaic Village in Middleboro, Massachusetts.* Special Publication of the Cohannet Chapter of the Massachusetts Archaeological Society, 1959.

Robbins, Maurice. *The Indian History of Attleboro.* Special Publication of the Attleboro Historical Commission, 1969.

Robbins, Maurice. *Wapanucket: An Archaeological Report.* Special

Publication of the Massachusetts Archaeolgical Society, 1980.

Robinson, Charles T. *"Culture Clash in Early New England."* **The Rehoboth Reporter.** January, 1991; 11-15.

Robinson, Charles T. *"A Few Fragments of Rehoboth Prehistory."* **The Rehoboth Reporter.** November, 1991; 15-20.

Russell, Howard S. *Indian New England Before The Mayflower.* Hanover: University Press of New England, 1980.

Simmons, William. *Spirit of the New England Tribes: Indian History and Folklore 1620-1984.* Hanover: University Press of New England, 1980.

Snow, Dean R. *The Archaeology of New England.* New York: Academic Press, 1980.

Speiss, Arthur E. Michaud: *A Paleo-Indian Site in the New England Maritimes Region.* Occasional Publications in Maine Archaeology- Number Six- Maine Archaeological Society and Maine Historic Preservation Commission, 1987.

Tilton, Rev. George H. *A History of Rehoboth, Massachusetts.* Boston: Published By The Author, 1918.

Waldman, Carl. *Atlas of the North American Indian.* New York: Facts On File Publications, 1985.

Whipple, Warren. Whipple, Marion. *The Story of Middleboro's Prehistoric Origins.* Published by the Authors, 1990.

Wilbur, C. Kieth. *The New England Indians.* Chester: The Globe Pequot Press, 1978.

Index